WHISPERS

Transforming Words for Your Ever-Changing Life

KIMBERLY MACNEILL

Author photo by Jen Jacobowitz Photography www.jenjacobowitz.com

WestBow Press books may be ordered through booksellers or by contacting:

WestBow Press
A Division of Thomas Nelson & Zondervan
1663 Liberty Drive
Bloomington, IN 47403
www.westbowpress.com
1 (866) 928-1240

ISBN: 978-1-4908-5056-6 (sc)
ISBN: 978-1-4908-5058-0 (hc)
ISBN: 978-1-4908-5057-3 (e)

Library of Congress Control Number: 2014915810

Printed in the United States of America.

WestBow Press rev. date: 09/26/2014

And I am certain that God, who began the good work within you, will continue his work until it is finally finished on the day when Christ Jesus returns.

(Philippians 1:6 NLT)

Contents

A Note from the Author

Maybe we have met before. Maybe we haven't. Maybe we know each other, or maybe we don't. You may be reading this book because you want to, or you may be reading it because someone encouraged you to do so. I don't know exactly how you and I met here, but I don't think it is an accident. God does stuff like that. And yes, I believe in God. If you don't, that's okay. I think this book still has something to say to you. But I do want you to know that I am a Christian, and I deeply believe that a life with God, under his watch and care, living according to his ways, is the best way to truly live.

So first, I'd like to tell you a little about that.

When I became a follower of Jesus, I had no idea what was ahead of me. As a child, I had been told that God loved me. I knew I was separated from him by my sin, and I knew that Jesus had died on the cross and was resurrected so that my sin might be forgiven—forever. The gap between God and humankind had been bridged by the cross: Jesus was the Savior of the world. But then came the moment in my life when I understood that I had a decision to make; Jesus was *the* Savior, but was he *my* Savior?

Asking Jesus to be my Savior was the best decision I ever made. The forgiveness from sin was welcomed in my life and I felt so new! A clean slate! A fresh start! I believed then that God's ways were best, and after thirty years of walking with God, I still do.

Looking back, I wished there were some things I had understood from the beginning. One, I wish I'd understood better this gift of new life God was giving me. Two, I wish I'd understood the process that was ahead of me. God was not *finished* with me on my day of salvation; this was just the *beginning*! There was more to come. My life was not just *changed*; it was going to be *changing*.

The Bible says that God makes all things new. And he does. He made me new the day I received his gift of salvation, and he continues to make me new on a daily basis. His love redeemed me in a moment of truth, and his love continues to restore me in constant moments of truth. This process of making us new is something only God can do, and he has his own ways of doing it. It is my prayer that the thoughts here will enlighten you to God's ways as you experience his work in and through you. If you are a Christian, your salvation isn't only a prepaid ticket to heaven; God wants you to have a life worth living! And if you are not a Christian, I hope you know that God wants the same for you.

A little bit about me: I have experienced life as a daughter, wife, aunt, spiritual mother, mini-mart cashier, pizza maker, high school English teacher, youth minister, missionary, creative director, worship artist, preacher, pastor, learner, and leader. And, I sold lingerie. I grew up in the East, lived in the West, and now reside in the South. I grew up on a rugged road called Whittengale, lived with a lady named Flossie, and rented a house on Dove's Nest Farm. I have traveled across the oceans to places I never thought I would see.

I love to teach the Bible. I love to tell stories. I try to be honest. I like to have fun and laugh. I want to drink coffee together, with you, in the morning and have tea in the afternoon, seeking and seeing God in every moment he gives us together. My passion is this: I am living *and* dying to inspire you. I believe he is calling your name, pursuing you, and changing you. I am hoping and expecting God to do something new in your life. I want you to take the next step in your spiritual journey, and I will do whatever God asks of me, whatever my part, to see that happen in your life.

I want to make creative contributions to God's work in the world—this book being just one of those. You should know I was afraid to write it, *and* I am afraid for you to read it. I am afraid of being misunderstood and criticized. And yet I am compelled to do it. I read this quote by Thomas Merton that said, "If a writer is so cautious that he never writes anything that cannot be criticized, he will never write anything that can be read. If you want to help other people you have got to make up your mind to write things that some men will condemn."

Yeah. That was not helpful.

I'm afraid you will read this and say to yourself that you can't believe this girl has both an English and a divinity degree, a gift of leadership and communication, and is a mainline, evangelical Christian. I'm afraid my family will be a little embarrassed by my stories, and I'm afraid my friends who thought we agreed on certain things will find out that we don't. And I'm really afraid that the book will just not be that good (I mean, I have never done this before)!

But, fear does not get to win.

Not long ago, a friend sat me down and told me that God had given her a vision, and she wanted to share it with me. Here is how it went. She said, "I see you flying. You are on an eagle ... flying! God is doing a work in your life. It is good *now*, and it is going to be good in the *future*."

Though I appreciated this encouragement, by my estimation, God was not at work in my life at all at the time. I couldn't see it.

Then she said, "But, there is an issue. You are straddling the eagle, leaned over, holding on to his neck for dear life. Kimberly, you are choking the eagle!"

Okay. Now *that* I could see.

In a commanding voice she said, "Stand up on the eagle's back, balance, and soar!"

And I thought to myself, *Yeah—I'm pretty sure that won't be happening. I'm afraid of heights. And I can't balance.* I pictured the boy in the movie *How to Train a Dragon* when he is riding the dragon. He is afraid, his eyes are wide, and he is crouched over gripping the dragon's neck. He is not confident that this is going to go well. Will they get where they want to go? Can he trust his winged friend?

Then the Scripture came to me: "But those who trust in the LORD will find new strength. They will soar high on wings like eagles. They will run and not grow weary. They will walk and not faint" (Isaiah 40:31 NLT).

And the Lord started stirring this story in my head until I heard his message in these words: *Kimberly, you can trust me. I will not let you fall. Yes, dips in altitude, moments of downward spiral may occur; straight-up vertical climbs might happen. But there will be no falling out of the sky, splattering on the ground. Get my perspective. Let my perspective be your perspective.*

God said, *Kimberly. Stand up so you can see things from my point of view.*

And so, I wrote this book.

Preface

The Butterfly Whisperer

It was a Sunday morning, and I was leading the weekend service.

I was preaching on the Christian life and the transformation that God intends for each of us. I love teaching on this topic so I can explain and remind people that God is at work in and through us. He is not done with us yet. Our day of salvation is only the beginning. He is constantly making all things new in our lives. And knowing that we all get lulled back into the world and lazy in our pursuit of God, I love to deliver a message that will inspire the believer to get excited again about the work of God in them.

One of the best illustrations of transformation is the butterfly. Most people know this, and it has been used a lot—maybe overused. But for this day, I didn't care. I decided to use it as the key, closing image of my message. And I decided to go big with it. I spent some money. I kept it a secret from most everyone except for the few people I needed to pull it off. I decided to do a butterfly release *inside* the auditorium.

As people arrived for the services, I gave out small boxes to one hundred different people; inside each one was a beautiful monarch. Each person was given the cue and asked to hide his or her box until it came time for the release. At the closing of the message, I talked about the transformation a butterfly goes through, and I released the first butterfly from my hands. And then, right on cue, a host more joined in flight. It was unexpected. It took people's breath away. It was inspiring! And we had all shared in that moment together.

During the second service, though, something happened. We had asked the first service attenders not to mention the moment to those entering for the second service, and we thought we had done a pretty good job clearing out the butterflies in between services, but apparently we did not get them all! Right in the middle of the second message—not yet to the topic of butterflies—one started flying around me on the platform.

You can imagine, people were delighted by this little butterfly that "just happened" to find its way inside the building. Of course, the big screen magnified the butterfly, and everyone could see clearly what was going on. I was trying to continue the message while acting like there was *not* a butterfly circling me. There came that moment when the butterfly had stolen the show, and I had to do something. So, acknowledging the butterfly, I spoke to it and invited it to circle me and land on the teaching table—*and it did.* It landed right on my Bible and rested there. The congregation audibly gasped in wonder and then broke out into spontaneous applause.

From then on, I was called The Butterfly Whisperer.

It was in this story that I found the purpose of this book. I am motivated to see lives changed, to see your life and my life transformed by God's power into the image of Christ. And in order to see that happen, I believe there are things we need to be aware of; things we need to know. And sometimes we need some coaching...maybe from a butterfly whisperer. We need people to come alongside us to teach, to mentor, to train, to encourage, to motivate, to believe in us; we need people who understand who we are and have a vision for what we can become in Christ. I have had people like this in my life, and at times God has allowed me to be that person for others. This book is full of words I have both heard and said: words that made a difference.

Transformation is not an easy process, I know, and sometimes it can be painful. Sometimes we can be confused when we are in the middle of some new thing God is doing in us. But, if we are aware of who God is and how he works, change can be a little less intimidating and a little more faith building. Our eyes can see a little more clearly and our hearts trust a little more deeply as God shapes and molds us.

In this book I hope you will find words of truth, hope, and love. I have found that sometimes truth is harder to hear when someone is shouting it, so I whispered it here. You will find quiet messages of hope because I know how hard it is to have such when hopelessness is so much more real. And as for the whispers of love, I hope you hear them deeply. I wrote them, but they are from God. For he is the one who knows you best and loves you most; he is the one with the plan and the purpose, the presence and the power to transform your life. He is the one who wonderfully made you in the beginning, and he is the one who can already see the beautiful creation you are becoming.

> And I am certain that God, who began the good work within you, will continue his work until it is finally finished on the day when Christ Jesus returns.
>
> (Philippians 1:6 NLT)

The Changing Life

A changed life is a changing life
And now that my life is changed
I have changes to make

NOW BEGINS THE JOURNEY

Unending love
Constant surrender
Enduring freedom

Loved where I am
Moved on by love
To who I will be

Redeemed
Restored
Realized

I am certain
I am convinced
I am sure
I am confident

He will continue
He will guide me along
He will keep at it
He will carry it through

He will teach me the way I should go
Where to go

The best pathway for my life

By Kimberly MacNeill, 2013

INTRODUCTION

Your Ever-Changing Life

Whether you are a Christian or not, you have probably heard that Jesus wants to change your life—and indeed, he does. In fact, he can and he will, if you want him to. But know this: once he changes it, he will keep on changing it. It is not a one-time thing.

> Put on your new nature, and be renewed as you learn to know your Creator and become like him.
>
> (Colossians 3:10 NLT)

Becoming a Christ-follower is just the beginning of God's work in our lives. He is continually making us new. He is continually urging us to let go of the selfish things in our lives that are not from him and leading us to embrace his goodness and grace as our own. The changing life is about transformation; it is the metamorphosis of your soul in God's hands. It is a series of transitions, some harder than others.

But, do not fear. God will provide for you whatever you need—courage, grace, endurance ... He will guide and empower you through every transition. *Old stuff* will die, yes, but you didn't need those things. The *new stuff* that God brings to your life will meet every need you have. The changes that God will make in your life are real—good, perfect, virtuous, and meaningful beyond your imagination.

Metamorphosis is hard. It is messy. There's the *before* and the *after.* The *former* and the *current.* The *certain past* and the *uncertain future.* The *wanted change* and the *unwanted change.* And there is the sometimes dreaded *between.* Trusting God is of paramount importance. In fact, it won't happen without him. But do note: it won't happen without *you.* Don't get stuck in self-rationalization and justification saying, "I can't change" and "I am who I am." This kind of thinking puts up a wall against who you can become in Christ. The question to ask yourself is not, Am I *able* to change? but, Am I *willing* to change?

Transformation, by experience, can be observed in the butterfly. As a caterpillar, the "to be" butterfly faces an obstacle in its metamorphosis: its skin cannot grow with it. So, at each significant transition, it has to grow another larger skin. Meaning, while it is living with one skin, it is always growing another underneath. When the new skin is ready, the caterpillar sheds the old skin. This process called "molting" happens five times. And in the last phase, the wings are actually forming underneath the skin before they are exposed.

Now, I don't know about you, but the whole thing sounds painful. And the whole idea that you have to go through it more than once, over and over again? I'm exhausted thinking about it! And if I were a soon-to-be butterfly, I think I might lose hope in the process. Yet, I can't imagine the world without butterflies. They are amazing! And they are *insects*! So, imagine you—a human being—created by God in his image, with a life that is growing and changing and becoming more and more like him ...

Transformation is a wonder of life you don't want to miss! To be the best of who you were created to be, to live out your purpose and significance, to live and thrive in the light of God forever and ever, and to be more like Jesus, full of love and grace. *You don't want to miss this.* I plead with you, let God's story be written in your life.

The making of your soul, the shape and substance of who you become matters because *you* matter. God created you in his image with a unique design. Plus, he placed within you common threads that you share with other members of humankind. He made us meaningful and beautiful. He gave us both passion and purpose. He filled you with love and grace and peace so that you could experience them for yourself, as well as share them with the world. He gifted you with life itself.

And inside this gift of life, our souls both soar and struggle. We are both strong and fragile. We have strengths and weaknesses. Words and events both build us up and drain us. Our souls can be harmed by choices and actions, and healed by the same. All of this is part of our beautiful, constantly changing life in him.

It might be said that we are cocreators of our lives with God. God does his part and we do ours. Yes, God is sovereign, but that does not mean we can abdicate responsibility for our own lives. We are not robots, puppets, or projects. We are living, breathing, creations of God, and each of us has a unique identity and place in this world. We have our own will, and God will not violate that. So, it is our decision about how we are going to grow and give, learn and live. And we are either going to cooperate with him or not. It is our choice.

I believe our souls thrive when we operate in communion with our Creator, the one who made us. He knows us best. More than that, he loves us most. We can trust him. Opening up to him and inviting him to move in our lives might be a struggle at first, but it really is a sweet surrender. Looking for him in people and places, listening for his voice, and committing to a deeper responsiveness to his leading are the keys to our spiritual formation. We cannot change and grow alone; we will become weary quickly if we rely on our own self-effort. We need the power of God.

Thus, we need the cross. It is our symbol of wholeness and hope. It tells our story of when we walked away from the soul-maker and brokenness was birthed; and it stands for the truth of our redemption and restoration, speaking of what is and will be in and through us. We hold on and we hold true to the extravagant love it represents, permeating every aspect of our lives; and we rely on the spiritual power that it pours forth and penetrates the entire universe in which we live.

The making of our souls is a journey of faith. We have a destiny. There are days when we have to believe in what we cannot see. There are many times when we ask God, like the kid in the car, "Are we there yet?" The fact is, we are going to need an eternal perspective for this journey; we are going to need to live today like forever has already begun.

Because it has.

WHISPER 1

Embrace and Experience Every Day of Your Life

Moments and Seasons

Feel the Day

My first full-time job was as a schoolteacher. Our campus was mostly enclosed, lunch was a mere twenty-three minutes, and I taught all day. From 7:30 a.m. till 3:30 p.m. I was in my classroom or chasing kids in the hallway. In the wintertime, I would arrive at school in the dark of morning, and by the time papers were graded at the end of the day, it was dark again when I left. I had missed the sun.

Inside the classroom, I was focused on the myriad things that needed to get done: lessons to be taught, papers to be filed, projects to be displayed. There never seemed to be enough time to get it all finished. Have you felt like that? Are you busy and rushed with a to-do list too long to fit inside the small window on the calendar labeled "TODAY"?

It was in one of the transitions between jobs that I had free days that were not labeled as "vacation." They were actually, simply, days where I had nothing to do. So, I decided to *feel the day*. I took my time, breathed in and out deeply all day long. I took time to notice that which was around me. I didn't rush or try to plan anything. I took note of the sun, its rising and setting. I actually tasted the food that I ate, and I listened to music and heard every lyric.

When I went to the store to get something, I greeted people one by one. I spent time reflecting on the week and on life itself. If I saw something at the house that needed to be done, I did it, enjoying the actual doing and the finishing of that small task. And I learned something: there is a lot of life in a single day. It doesn't matter whether it is a free day or the busiest workday of the year. Each day is full of meaning; each day is a time frame inspired by and full of God.

So now I try to *feel the day* every day: see the sun, hear the music, talk to people one by one, work and play with all my might. I welcome any challenge and receive any surprises. I even check out the moon before bedtime. And all the while, in between, I experience the textures of the day that may come as tears, laughter, frustration, peace, confusion, gratitude, faith, pain, or wonder. It is in an ordinary day that defining moments take place. And when those days are strung together, I can see seasons of growth in my life.

Defining Moments and Seasons of Growth

I believe there are times of revelation in our lives, times when God reveals himself to us. We experience his presence, witness his power, and encounter truth. I also believe there are times of conversion in our lives when we experience a change of mind and a change of heart. We think differently. We act differently. Both revelation and conversion can happen in a moment; but, they can also take a whole season of time.

The moments that make a soul can be ones we simply witness from the outside or moments we are actually part of. Something happens—someone says something or does something. Or it could be me and you. We say something or do something that we didn't know was in us. And it could be good or it could be wrong. But somehow, some way, that moment mattered. It touched us deeply. It gave us a new perspective as it taught us a lesson. The interesting thing is that as meaningful as that moment was to us, we probably didn't see it coming.

Seasons are different. They take time—more time than we think or want them to take. We might have seen them coming, but we surely have no idea when they will end. There is a lot of waiting and wondering: Why? What? When? Sometimes there is a definitive moment when we see the purpose of it all, and we see how we have grown. But more often, the season passes, and gradually we see that God did change us and grow us. Even if we couldn't feel it or see it, we find ourselves now different.

Moments: Small, but Mighty

Moments are small but mighty points in time. They are like a person short in stature with the presence of a king. They are like the football player who is smaller but faster. Moments come and go quickly, yet they have a lifelong impact on us. When we take time to experience them, we are more in tune with what God is doing in us and around us. Some moments are teachable ones, some are life-affirming, and some break us. Whatever kind of moment it is, we live to our fullest when we embrace it rather than ignore it.

Moments come in both good news and bad news, decisions and indecisions, answers of yes and no, confessions and reconciliations: You got the job. They are getting a divorce. The adoption is final. The jury is split. You say "I do." The bank says "no." A truth is spoken. A lie is told. Forgiveness is granted. These and millions of defining moments like them are not to be missed. The richest person in life is the one who embraces them.

I attended a conference once where Dewitt Jones, a top professional photographer for *National Geographic* magazine was speaking. An intimate gathering was held for him, and I was invited. I sat down at the table with my plate and before I knew it, he plopped down beside me. It was a great experience to dialogue with him one on one. As we discussed art and photography, I asked him what he felt was the key to taking great pictures. And he told me this: "*The key to taking great pictures, capturing beauty, is not in the framing of the shot, not in the lighting, and not in the lens. The key to taking great pictures is about snapping the shot in the right moment. It's about being there.*"

Upon further reflection, I took his words to heart: If you want to capture and experience the beauty and abundance of your life, you are going to have to "be there" in the moments that come your way.

Ah-Ha Moments

Ah-ha moments are when you finally *get* something you didn't *get* before. A learning. A moment of clarity out of confusion. I have been to a lot of conferences where the teaching has led me to ah-ha moments. Finally, the speaker explained something to me that I had been trying to understand, or God spoke to me through the speaker on a personal matter that I had been struggling with.

The most significant time this happened to me was when I was thirteen years old. For me, becoming a Christian was an ah-ha moment. The reason was that I had never understood it was a choice for me to make. I had equated faith and family, not understanding that *I* was invited to choose Jesus and place my faith in him to be my Savior. Jesus knew *me* and *my* name, and he had a plan for *my* life. Faith was personal, and my relationship with God unique! As a result of that moment, I chose to follow Christ.

Another ah-ha moment came for me when I committed to reading the Bible in ninety days. Spending day after day in the Old Testament I gained a glimpse of what it was like for people to wait for the Messiah. And then, when I turned the last page of Malachi and began to read the first page of Matthew, I felt like I was experiencing my salvation all over again! Jesus had come! The breathtaking truth of the gospel was real to me again that day.

How about you? Have you had any ah-ha moments in your life?

"Wonder-Full" Moments

Some moments shock the heart: if it was beating too slow it speeds up, and if it was beating too fast it slows down. These are moments of full of wonder. I heard someone say that the definition of *wonder* is "allowing life to kiss you unexpectedly." I have never forgotten that statement, and like a true romantic, I have since wished for lots of kisses!

One of those kisses, for me, came in a hospital. Though I have never given birth to a baby myself, I had the privilege of being in the room when one of my nephews was born. All the pain and drama and waiting of labor, and then all of the sudden, there he was! He just slipped right out of my sister-in-law's body! I mean, I'm sure it didn't feel like that to her, but it sure did seem that way from where I was standing! That one moment alone schooled me in the sanctity of life. The actual creation of this thing called "life" was truly more amazing for me after that.

How about you? Have you had any wonder-full moments in your life?

Life-Breaking Moments

Sometimes things happen that aren't fair, things that seem too horrible for people to go through. We experience moments that are full of sorrow, injustice, chaos, and fear. They interrupt and disrupt; these moments turn life upside down in a way that we don't want them to. But they define us. And if given into the Lord's hands, they can be redeemed for good purpose.

I had a friend die of leukemia at age forty-one. I was in the room when she took her last breath; it was like time stood still. I realized that in the same moment while I was watching her exhale her last breath on earth, she was in heaven breathing in her first sight of Jesus. I never looked at life the same again. We all say we should live each day like it is our last, but on a daily basis I think we forget to do so. I try harder now, not to forget.

That life-breaking moment was one I shared in with a community of people. We all struggled with losing our friend, but God redeemed it all. Our community was resilient. Our faith wavered at first and then grew beyond our own doing. We are different because of her life and death. Life-breaking moments are not the kind we wish for, but they happen. And they can change us for the good.

How about you? Have you had any of these life-breaking moments?

Life-Affirming Moments

There are moments in *life* that actually breathe *life* into one's *life*. (That's a lot of *life*.) And without them, we would probably be dead. Really. Maybe not physically, but emotionally and spiritually, we would be goners. Everyone needs life-affirming moments, so when one comes your way, never take it for granted. You actually *need* it.

My licensing to the ministry was a life-affirming moment for me. Upon voicing my calling to the leadership, I was vetted and then approved. It was a spring evening when a worship service was held to seal the deal. At the service, my pastor preached on the topic of women in ministry and the scriptural basis of the "setting apart" for a vocational life in ministry. It was a hot topic on a cool evening!

With all of the pastoral staff of the church plus one other, they encircled me, laid hands on my shoulders, and prayed for me. Recognizing my gifts and calling, they affirmed my life publicly and commissioned me to be my best and do my best for God always, as a worker and a leader, ultimately a servant to his church. To be seen for whom God had made me was soul-nourishing. To be accepted by my peers was encouraging. To be loved by a community of believers and to serve them with my life was invigorating. This life-affirming moment was one that refueled me over and over again in my life of ministry.

What have been life-affirming moments for you?

Seasons: Longer and Deeper (and Often Harder)

Seasons are the sum of moments. But to embrace and experience a season is a whole different ball game than living a moment—plain and simple, seasons are longer. Good seasons are the best-ever times of life. Day after day you get a front seat to great things happening in your life. So many things you prayed for come to be. Joy and contentment are at your fingertips. A good season is like summertime: everything is bright, in full-bloom, and flourishing.

Then there is that less-than-good season, like fall. Things that were so vibrant and healthy have run their course and started to wither. It's a season of life when things are okay, but you feel like you are on a downward slope. And then there are times of life when it feels like the dead of winter—no life, no color. Everything seems to have died. The landscape of life is frozen and desolate. It seems like nothing good will ever happen again.

And just when you think you can't take it anymore, a new season emerges and something new pops up out of nowhere. A tree twig births a bud. A blade of grass pops through the dirt. A butterfly wing begins to form. You have hope again: God is going to do something new. The fact is, it takes all of these seasons and the time in between to appreciate each one. Embracing and experiencing one season makes all the difference in the next. We will have a deeper understanding of life as well as openhandedness with the mystery of it if we will do so.

The summers and springs of life don't call for much discussion, as they are times of celebration and fruitfulness. It is the falls and winters of life that are harder to grasp and live through. Here, I have chosen to unearth a few things I have learned about latter.

In 2001, Bruce Wilkinson wrote the book *Secrets of the Vine.*[1] The content of the book centered on the gospel of John, chapter 15, when the Last Supper took place with Jesus and his disciples. Jesus spoke truths to the believers in that room, and these truths still matter to believers today. Over the years I kept that book near and dear, and it helped me understand many things. But there was one thing Wilkinson and I disagreed on: while he called these truths "secret," I found them to be "not so secret."

I suppose I was under the impression like him that spiritual growth would be a hush-hush matter. But, in fact, once you start experiencing life "in the vine," your soul is downright exposed and brought into the light; there is nothing confidential or classified about it. It is not subtle nor is it peacefully paced. Sure, God is at work *within* you, but believe me when I say others can sense it and see it, and you can feel it. Growing requires a stretching and changing of shape and consistency, and it is not easy.

It is not-so-secret.

Divine Pruning

In the Central Valley of California, landscaping looks pretty good all year long. Sure, there is a winter season, though people in the East would never call *that* winter! I mean, there is no snow, no wind chill, and no ice. But it does get rainy and gloomy and "chilly." (and when it gets chilly, even if it is still seventy degrees, everyone gets out their fur-lined boots) The bottom line is that your backyard always looks pretty good, the grass is mostly green, and you can still have some flowers. You can imagine that if it is like this in the winter, the spring is spectacular! I loved it when the bushes were full and everything was in bloom.

So many mornings I would turn to my husband and say, "Our backyard is beautiful!" And without a doubt—like clockwork—the gardener would come that afternoon and prune everything. It never failed! Just when I thought the purple fountain grass was looking its best, the gardener cut it; just as it was covering the air conditioner, nicely hiding that electronic box, he whisked it away. It was a big disappointment to come home that evening after work and see things minimized. I knew it had to be done, but it bothered me. The beauty was gone and it looked so bare. Each time, my husband would have to remind me of how much better it would look later. But I didn't care about later. It had been good enough for me that morning.

I realize that's how I feel about my life sometimes. I can hit a new spiritual stride and feel closer to the Lord than ever before with my life bearing fruit, full and lush ... and then "clip," the Master Gardener does some pruning. I know pruning is a good thing, and I know it has to be done, but it discourages me. There ensues the same scenario as the purple fountain grass: just when I think my life in the Lord is flourishing, God prunes it in some way and my husband reminds me of how much better life will be later. But, it's hard for me to see a bare spot in an area where my life once flourished. I know that God has a vision for who he making me to be and I do trust him. It's just that the "clip" part hurts and feels like a loss. My prayer, though, is that I will not be satisfied with less or be comfortable in my estimation of what is "good enough." I want to go as far as God will take me.

One important thing I have tried to remember is this: the gardener's hand is closest to the plant when he is pruning it. He reaches in close to the root, his eyes focused on the place to be pruned, and with discernment and gentleness he makes the cut. The Master Gardener does the same. In the process of pruning, it may seem that God is not present, but in fact, he is very close to you. His loving hand is near. His eyes are focused on you.

> I am the true grapevine, and my Father is the gardener. He cuts off every branch of mine that doesn't produce fruit, and he prunes the branches that do bear fruit so they will produce even more.
>
> (John 15:1–2 NLT)

The purpose of all this is so that our lives will produce *more* fruit. Pruning can feel punishment; you wonder if you did something wrong. But pruning happens because your life *is* thriving. You are not getting pruned because God is not in your life; you are being pruned because God *is* in your life. The pruning is not a consequence to your sin; it is a blessing because of your faithfulness. Truly, God is not seeking to take something away from you. Pruning happens because God wants to give you more.

In fact, if a tree is particularly fruitful, bearing fruit at an ultimate capacity, it must be pruned because if not, the weight of the fruit will become too much for the branches as they are. A tree like this is pruned at a thicker segment of the branch so that the new growth will make the tree stronger to prepare it to live up to its next stage of fullest potential, which is *even more* than before!

But they say to prune that tree at a thick part of the branch is a tough cut to make. It's not a clip from shears: it takes a full-blown saw to make that prune. So you can imagine, if we are talking about the spiritual life, and if you are living a fruitful Christian life and God decides to prune you for an even greater future, that prune is going to hurt. That loss is going to begin a rough season of life. It will take every ounce of faith for you to stay connected, living in the Vine, allowing time for change and growth in you, allowing time to regain strength. And without a doubt, you will need faith to trust God that there is a future ahead for you.

Over the years, I have taken several trips to Minnesota (talk about winter!), and on one of them I visited a city zoo. In one of the lush garden areas stood a fig tree. It looked dead as a doornail, and I wondered why they left it there. As I got closer, I found a sign posted by it saying

Why Was the Fig Tree Pruned?
To Encourage New Growth
Because It Only Blooms and Develops
New Fruit on New, Annual Growth.
This Type of Pruning Is Called
Pollarding.

I was glad this dead-looking fig tree had a sign, otherwise people like me would have written it off at first sight. Those of us lacking understanding needed an explanation of why this tree stood seemingly lifeless. For us, in a season of pruning, we will probably resemble this tree and wish we could wear a sign around our necks, too, so that people understand what is going on in our lives. More so, we might need a sign that we can look at to remind *ourselves* where we are in our spiritual formation. I need to be reminded that God is at work, and he does have a plan, and he is indeed doing a good work in me; he *is* making me new.

Have you ever experienced a “pruning” in your life? What was the result?

Apple Trees and Chill Seasons

Did you know that apple trees have a “chilling requirement”? A period of cold weather has to happen before the tree will blossom.

Basically, the tree becomes dormant to protect itself from the cold weather, and it needs to stay there until spring has truly arrived with enough sunshine for the blossoms to thrive. If it blossoms too soon, and a late frost comes, the tree could be hindered from its full potential for fruit that season.

So what?

Some seasons of life are intended to protect us. God is the one with the whole picture, and we have to trust in that. He is the one with the master timing, the master calendar. He knows when and why we need to be "dormant" for a while, and he knows when it is the best time for us to "bloom" again.

Have you ever been able to look back and see that God gave you a certain season in order to protect you?

Those Orange Trees

One of the most important aspects of a tree is that which is not seen: the roots.

There is a story told by a pastor who visited an orange grove and was given a tour by the orchardist himself. Passing by some trees that were beginning to die due to lack of water, the orchardist explained that an irrigation pump had broken down during this unusually dry season.

Moving on, the man took the pastor to another orchard where irrigation was used sparingly. He said, "These trees could go without rain for another two weeks. You see, when they were young, I frequently kept water from them. This hardship caused them to send their roots deeper into the soil in search of moisture.

Now, these are the deepest-rooted trees in the area. While others are being scorched by the sun, these are finding moisture at a greater depth."

The truth is, sometimes God allows harder things in our lives so that our "roots of faith" will grow deeper. And once we have deeper roots, there is no season of circumstance or challenge that we can't make it through and overcome. The transformation he is working in our lives is to build our strength and resilience; he is making us strong and courageous in him.

Waiting and Fruit Salad

I was on my way out of town, moving to a new city, and a friend took me aside with some urgency. She felt the Lord had given her a message for me that I needed to hear before I left. She said, "There are times coming when you will feel that your life is not bearing fruit. You will look down into your basket, and it will be empty: no souls won to the Lord, no ministry wins, no blessings to be received or given. Though it is only temporary, you will have a hard time with it. And to make matters more difficult, everyone around you will be bearing so much fruit, leading such plentiful lives in the Lord that they will be making fruit salad! And there you will be with an empty basket *and* an empty bowl. You will wonder what the Lord is doing. When that time comes, just wait on the Lord. He will direct your path to what's next and make your life fruitful again."

All of what she said came true. And as a type A, driven individual, it was the hardest season of my life. I felt unsuccessful; unaccomplished; and more so, lacking purpose. I was jealous of others and envied their flourishing lives in every aspect. Everyone seemed right in the center of God's will, serving the Lord with enthusiasm; everyone seemed to have God's favor. Except me. After so many years of preparation and experience for what I thought would be the best years of my life, there I stood, with an empty basket and an empty bowl, just waiting.

I don't know about you, but I am not a good "wait-er." I am impatient, and I doubt. My trust wavers. My belief falters.

Maybe you are in a season of waiting. Waiting for Mr. Right? Waiting for the woman of your dreams? Waiting for a promotion to launch your career? Waiting for a financial windfall? Waiting for a physical or emotional healing? Waiting for direction from the Lord in any matter? Well, here's something you need to know.

Waiting is an actual *activity*. Meaning, it is *active*. In both the Old and New Testaments the meaning of *waiting* is "standing under, actively enduring." It is not standing with our arms folded in passive resignation doing nothing. When we wait, we engage our strength to stand, knowing God is there, enduring till the answer comes. We have hope. Our eyes are not closed; they are wide open, looking attentively to see what God is doing and will do. The question is not *if* God will come through; the question is *when*?

And though we don't want to have expectations, we do want to wait expectantly. We anticipate that God will show up. Understanding what it means to wait in the biblical sense makes all the difference as we are molded and changed into the image of Christ. As God works out his will in our lives, we will often find ourselves in a *waiting pattern*, but this is not the same as being in a *holding pattern*.

Pursue the Lord while you wait. Continue to do good works in his name. Wake up every morning looking to see if this is the day God will do the new thing you are waiting for. Wait with great hope!

Whisper 1: Embrace and Experience Every Day of Your Life

Can you hear this, my whisper to you? *Embrace and experience every day of your life.* When it's good, when it's hard, when it's glorious, when it's excruciatingly painful ... somehow, some way, receive it as the gift that it is. Moments and seasons are the time frames by which our souls are shaped and fulfilled by the Spirit of God. He is in each one, at work, according to his greater purpose.

When he takes you deeper, go there. When the day comes and you enter into the forever season of heaven, I pray you will find that it is not that different from where you have already been. Why? Because you have already been abiding in God so closely, for so long, through so many seasons that there will be only one last thing to happen: you will see his face.

WHISPER 2

Remember, You Are Never Alone

Presence and Wonder

Present Presence

As I have said, my faith is a Christian faith, and it is a simple one. I believe in Jesus as my Savior, and I seek to live my life according to the Bible. Some people outside of the Christian life see it as restrictive and joyless. But for me, that "narrow road" as it is called, is not dry, nor is it boring. In fact, I find it full of presence and possibility.

People say they want to "live life" and experience all it has to offer. I wish that were how people understood the path of following God. I'm discouraged and saddened when I hear people say they are not interested in God's "restraints and limitations." It is hard to convince the spiritually blind that a life following God is the more compelling, richer choice. With him the possibilities are endless. With him the joy of living is at its fullest.

Since moving to the southeast, I have heard people talk about getting "beyond the pavement." They are actually saying, "Let's get out of town, down by the river, away from daily life as we know it." It means, let's break from the routine aspects of life that are drying up the joy of actually living.

The first time I heard that phrase, I realized that's what I'm hoping for in my walk with Christ. I want to get "beyond the pavement." There are routines to my faith that mean a lot to me: I attend a weekly gathering, I try to read the Bible daily, I pray, and I serve others. These are things I know and understand. But I want to know more of God. I want to hear his voice in fresh ways and obey him even if it takes risk. I want to brave the borders of the yet unknown that God has for my life.

The Bible tells us that God is both accessible to be known, *and* a mystery yet to be fully understood. I want to experience both. We spend a lot of time seeking to know God, and we ought to. To approach life with open eyes as he reveals himself to us makes every day an adventure and a deeper experience. I want to know him. But, I don't want to put him in a box. I mean, he still wouldn't fit into the biggest box I can imagine! And I certainly don't want to boil him down to a list of attributes and services. Nor do I want to be limited by words to express who he is.

Now, make no mistake. I need the pavement. I need what I can already see of God. Lists and words do help me understand who he is. I need the local church I can worship with and serve, the teaching of Scripture, and community and accountability with Christian brothers and sisters. These things keep me solid and strong in the daily living of my life for God. But with these things, if I'm not mindful, I will miss out on the mystery and the undefined, indescribable presence of God that is "beyond the pavement." If I'm not careful, my faith will become a mere routine that I barely think about with any depth.

I want to experience that sacred wonder of his presence; to encounter the mystery of the one I call Father and Savior and Spirit. I want to reside in the space and tension of what we do know about God and what we have yet to understand ... and be able to rest there.

Resting in a space of tension is not easy, and it is often avoided unknowingly—and sometimes knowingly. We spend most of our time trying to get out of spaces like this. In fact, it doesn't even make sense to say "rest" and "tension" in the same sentence. But, that's what I mean. In this space is growth. In this space is that peace that passes all understanding the Bible talks about. We are in the middle of what is and what will be; we are in the middle of what God has already revealed and what he will reveal. We are not sure what we will find in God, but we trust him and we know he is good.

I have seen people become enticed by New Age philosophies and practices. They find it interesting and meaningful. Why? Because it speaks to a need they have that the Christian church is not meeting: the need for the spiritual, for a sense of presence and not just information. People are looking for a touch of their soul, not just their minds and intellect. Most of the time, though, they are unaware of the dangerous waters they are stepping into. Just because the author or speaker talks of God, this does not mean he or she is talking about the one true God. If that person's faith is not in Jesus, and the lessons are not from the Bible, then buyer beware.

For me, my study of Scripture has led me to what many would call a conservative theology, and I have chosen to belong to churches of the same. Now, here is my sticky observation: I can see that churches like mine are uncomfortable with the Holy Spirit. The work of the Spirit is hard to explain, therefore hard to teach. The presence of the Spirit is hard to define, therefore hard to talk about. I have sometimes felt that the church is afraid of the Spirit simply because we don't know how to talk about him.

The church has worked hard to teach that faith is not a feeling. We worked so hard to teach this that we took all the feeling out of it. With good intentions, we did not want people to embrace Christianity based on emotion, nor did we want them to ride life on the waves of emotion. Who God is on a given day or in a given circumstance is not based on how we feel that day.

Out of fear that a philosophy of positive thinking would replace sound theology, we were very careful. We so much wanted people to have a solid faith that we kind of sucked the life out of being a Christian. We made faith cold, when in fact it is warm. We talked like God is emotionless, when in fact he is an emotional being and has made us in his image. We are created to feel him, to sense his presence. We are created to hear his voice and sense his promptings. And though we might not be able to explain every movement of the Spirit, we can test it to determine if it could possibly be him. Remember:

- Any mystery of God that you encounter will not dispute the Bible. It will corroborate it.
- Any voice you hear that is his will not contradict the Bible. It will agree.
- Any touch of his presence that you experience will not oppose the Bible. It will affirm.
- Any word a person speaks on behalf of God will not conflict with the Bible. It will align.

Our relationship with God was intended to be full of faith, and with faith comes the unknown, and the unknown to us is, yes, a mystery. But we don't have to be fearful. We have God's Word. No need to be nervous. We have his Spirit. Here is my desire: I want to experience all of God, not just what I can explain in my own words. I want to know of him that which I cannot find words for.

I don't need a life I can orchestrate on my own common sense and a little bit of God's wisdom; I want a life that goes deeper and travels wider than that. I want the life that Jesus talked about—abundant, gushing with love, and bursting at the seams with joy. That life that's chock-full of grace and surging with a peace that passes all human understanding. That one. The life that is empowered and transformed to be more like my great God.

So until that day when I see God face-to-face, I intend to love and pursue him with both my eyes and heart wide open. I commit to rest in the tension of mystery. I will not be afraid. I will live by faith, surrendered to his continuous, loving work in my life. For in this changing life he has given me, I will remember that I am not alone.

SADD: Spiritual Attention Deficit Disorder

Leighton Ford in his book *The Attentive Life* talks about SADD: Spiritual Attention Deficit Disorder.[2] We become easily bored with our faith, easily sidetracked from the one who matters most. Distractions dashing by catch our attention, and the next thing we know, we are off on a tangent, our focus blurred in the chase.

More so, though, our culture is the real deterrent to us paying attention to God. The world around us is hurried - most of the time for the wrong reasons. All of that scurry is not focused on getting us more of God; really, it is intent on us being more self-focused. Can you relate to what I'm saying here? Do you suffer from SADD? I do. There are some days when I will do anything but read my Bible, and other days when I could spend time praying and "being" with the Lord, but I end up checking things off my to-do list instead. Why is it that the things necessary for me to focus on and live out my faith are not at the top of my to-do list? Why isn't God number one when it comes to the priority of the day?

I don't know if you or I will ever get over our SADD, but I believe we can take steps to modify our behavior. We can have a plan that keeps our minds and bodies focused and gaining strength for a lifetime. If we are hoping for transformation in our lives, we will need to live in the awareness of God's presence. We need to be ready to hear him and follow him. A. W. Tozer says it best.

> The world is perishing for lack of the knowledge of God and the Church is famishing for want of His presence. The instant cure of most of our religious ills would be to enter the Presence in spiritual experience, to become suddenly aware that we are in God and God is in us. This would lift us out of our pitiful narrowness and cause our hearts to be enlarged.[3]

My life verse is Psalm 16:11: "You will show me the way of life, granting me the joy of your presence and the pleasures of living with you forever" (NLT). I chose this a long time ago, and it has kept me on track with the Lord. It helped me know early and live in the understanding that my life wasn't going to be all about his plan for what I would do and be on earth. My life with God was a forever one that started in the now, eternally characterized by the joy of his presence with me. No matter what happens in our lives, no matter the circumstances, he is with us. There is no greater gift. And there is no greater thing we need for our ever-changing life in God.

Sacred Wonder

On a recent plane flight, the captain gave a face-to-face greeting to the passengers. It was a rare occasion to receive a real-life, personal greeting from the pilot! He was quite warm, confident, and hospitable. At the end of his speech, he acknowledged a young boy who was seated in the last-row window seat. Apparently the boy had been touring the cockpit earlier, and this was his first ride on an airplane. Most of the passengers turned around to see the little boy, but only the tips of his fingers could be seen above the seat as he waved. Everyone buckled in and the plane began to taxi.

An excited voice rose above the noise, and you could hear him asking his dad, "Are we on the runway yet? Are we on the runway yet?" Then, when it finally came time for take-off, the plane started to speed up, and the boy began squealing with wonder and delight, shouting, "Here we go! Here we go!" As the plane lifted off the ground, the boy burst into gleeful laughter—uncontrollable happiness! Looking around, it was easy to see that everyone had a smile on his or her face.

The boy just could not get over the wonder and delight of flying on an airplane. Certainly most everyone else had flown before, and more than likely they were thinking about the cost and inconvenience of it, as well as the three hours of boredom ahead of them. But not this boy. He reminded everyone of the privilege and joy it is to fly. The fact that something this size can move through the air and take us places we once only dreamed of was not lost on this boy.

Our wonderful God gives us the gift of life with so much to enjoy! It can be easy to become too familiar with "wonder-full" experiences; sometimes we tend to see life as only "the same ole same ole." And yet, God gives us a new day every day. If we will wake up looking for God in fresh ways, we will see him in new ways. And if we keep our eyes open, we will find him in places we never thought we would. He is everywhere.

The Attentive Life

Keeping your eyes open and your awareness sharp can be a challenge. We all get distracted or slide into a lull at times, and we can get easily bored with the same old stuff in our lives. We can get so used to things that we take them for granted, forgetting how wonderful it is to have food and clothing and good health. We stop saying we love people because we assume they know—after all, we see them every day!

You know what I'm talking about: if you look at something long enough, before you know it you stop seeing it altogether. This happens with life itself. We kind of get used to it. And it happens with God when we kind of get used to him. And the next thing you know, we are missing out on seeing and experiencing the movements of God in our daily lives.

The subtitle of Ford's book is *Discerning God's Presence in All Things.* He talks about two practical ways we can do this, and these have made a big a difference in my life. When I have practiced them, I felt less alone and more centered in the reality that God is with me 24/7.

The first thing Leighton says to do is "look long enough."[4] So often we are so busy we just breeze by something God is doing to get to something we are doing. If we would just take a moment to look at something a little longer, we would see what God is up to there. People like to say that God doesn't sweat the small stuff, but I think we need to remember that he *is in* the details. God's work is handcrafted and intricate. You have to look long enough to see the beauty he is weaving so perfectly in each stitch; you have to look long enough to appreciate each paint stroke of his life-sized canvas. His presence is all around. He has created and is whipping up wonder all around us all the time!

The second thing Leighton says is to "look freshly at what is familiar."[5] Once we have seen something again and again, our eyes can essentially glaze over, and before you know it, we are not sure what it even looks like anymore. Having a certain comfort level with something or someone can be a good thing, but we can at times get *too* comfortable. We might no longer see the inherent value of something, or we might forget how much someone means to us.

This is when we need to take a *fresh* look. Take a moment, forget everything you already know, and try and see something for the first time. Rediscover the value and its meaning as God intended. Wonder is part of the abundant life. You don't want to miss it. Wonder reminds us of the beauty and the grandeur and the marvel of God. Wonder is what keeps us in that space of amazement and astonishment of the great God of the universe.

Whisper 2: Remember, You Are Never Alone

God is both immanent and transcendent. He knows the smallest details of everything and has the big picture, too. He has both a microscopic view and a helicopter perspective. Psalm 33:13–15 (NLT) says, "The Lord looks down from heaven and sees the whole human race. From his throne he observes all who live on the earth. He made their hearts, so he understands everything they do."

Within these two attributes is a tension in which you live—a good tension. God's holiness and sovereignty hold you reverently distant from him, while the love and mercy of God draw you to him. You respond to both of these forces. While God is anywhere and everywhere, he is also here with you. This is so important for you to remember as you grow in your faith. To understand that he is transcendent will help you to believe he is indeed as powerful as he claims, and quite capable and trustworthy with your life. To know that he is immanent, near you, shows you that he does indeed love you unconditionally and know you completely. The making of your soul takes place within these two realms of knowing God. He is with you in every way.

Whisper 3

Pay Attention to Where You Are and Who You Are With

People and Places

People

We need people. And we need all kinds of people. The people in my life who have been part of my spiritual formation have not all been Christians themselves. Some have been seekers still looking for God. Some have written God off and yet been good friends to me and taught me so much. But with that said, there is no question that a community centered on the Spirit of God working in and through it is essential to our transformation. We need the strength and love that come from being together with brothers and sisters in Christ. We need oneness with other journey-makers.

And, we need a few true friends and their words of encouragement, wisdom, and truth spoken in love. At times we will need their strength. Other times we will need their correction. They are the ones to call us out when we puff up with pride, to call us in when we wander off, and to call us to grace and healing when we need it.

We Need Each Other

Her name is Charlee. My niece. She is three years old going on thirteen—and some days thirty-three. Full of personality and opinion, she has an imagination that is hard for the adults to follow. One minute we are all in the living room, and the next minute she tells us we're at school. And we all do as the teacher says!

Every Thursday her grandma watches her. And on that day, Grandma's brother comes to visit. He always brings a plastic baggy with some coins in it. He hides them in the living room so she can find them. When she does, she runs off to get her piggy bank. Her bank has been full many times considering she is only three years old. Each time it is filled, Grandma rolls the coins and takes them to the bank. Since it was happening pretty often, Grandma got Charlee a new piggy bank—a bigger pig. She could barely get her arms around it.

One day, she came out of her bedroom hugging the piggy, and she carefully proceeded to the kitchen to show it off to a guest. But it was just too much for her to handle. She dropped the piggy bank, and it shattered all over the floor.

There was a moment of silence and shock. Her face squinted, and then came a flood of tears and an outcry of sadness. It was awful. Here was her treasure, and in that moment she thought she had lost it all. The piggy was broken, the money was scattered, and everyone was watching.

This whole thing happened to Charlee, but I felt like it happened to me. My heart felt her pain. Her outcry of despair and embarrassment penetrated my very being. I wondered, Why did I feel so deeply about what happened to her? And then I realized that the event resonated with me—I have actually felt those emotions before. I have held a treasure in my hands—a friendship, an opportunity, a blessing of some sort—and in a moment I dropped it and it "broke." I lost my opportunity and squandered my blessing. I didn't do it on purpose; it just happened. I was startled and sad and afraid all at the same time. And for me, more than that, I was embarrassed. There were people watching.

Maybe you can relate. Maybe you have had something that you treasured—a job, a family, a best friend, a ministry—and it slipped out of your hands; you dropped it. It was an accident, and you weren't planning on the whole thing shattering to pieces, but it did. And your friends saw it happen—and there wasn't anything they could do to stop it.

At Charlee's outcry, we rushed to her side. I picked her up and held her, stroking her hair. Grandma gathered the pieces of the piggy bank. Great Uncle gathered all the coins. Soon after, a new piggy bank was purchased. When I think of that response, I have to ask myself if the church would do the same. I hope so. I hope we would rush to the person's side to hold him or her and give comfort. I hope we would pick up the broken pieces surrounding these people and gather their scattered treasure. Though we can't "fix" situations like this, we can respond with love and grace. And if we will stick close long enough, we will get to see the new thing God does next: we will see beauty come from the ashes.

Kiss-and-Cry Section

If you have ever watched the figure skating competition in the Olympics, you have witnessed the "box" where the skater waits to find out their score/ranking. In that box is a team of people who support the competitor. They call it the Kiss and Cry section. If the skater scores well, they will all celebrate together. If he or she doesn't do well, they will cry together.

My friend Liz sits in this section of my life. When I do well with something, she celebrates with me rather than being jealous of me. When I have failed, she cries an empathetic, consoling cry with me rather than pointing a finger at my mistake. We have been through thick and thin together. She gave me a necklace once that said, "A True Friend Is Someone Who Knows The Song In Your Heart and Can Sing It Back To You When You Have Forgotten The Words." Her knowledge of me has at times been better than I know myself, and her support unwavering. What would I do without the Lizzies in my life?

Who is sitting in your Kiss-and-Cry section?

Balcony People

My friend Bryan gave me a book called *Balcony People* and honored me by saying he was one of mine. At the time, I barely knew him. He explained that a balcony person is one who watches you and cheers you on. When you doubt yourself, you can look for them and they will give you a nod of affirmation and a thumbs-up for encouragement. They are your cheerleaders.

Bryan has indeed been a balcony person for me. Not only did he give me the book, he has been there for me. He has cheered me on when I felt tired. He has commiserated with me over problems I could not fix and people I could not please, and he has given me a vote of confidence anyways. During my worst performances as a leader, he remained seated in the balcony and applauded my efforts nonetheless. I might have quit if it weren't for Bryan.

Who is sitting in your balcony?

Teammates

It had been eighteen months since I resigned from the church staff to relocate for my husband's new job. I assumed God would have something for me in our new city, too, and I was willing to wait in faith to find out what that was when we got there. But nothing substantial presented itself. Being more an introvert than an extrovert and often enjoying solo projects, I was surprised when I realized one of the things I missed most about being on a church staff was being on a team. I *really* missed working and serving with a team.

Though over the years the teams shifted in the "who" and the "what," I was still always part of a group of people who were doing something significant together. And yes, sometimes for the introverted part of me it was too much. Sometimes my team drove me crazy. I would think to myself, *No, I don't want to have coffee in the morning with you, work all day with you, eat two more meals with you, and then go to the movies to let off the steam of the day with you. And certainly I don't want to play golf on Saturday with you for "fun, relationship building" time.* I mean, it was just too much sometimes! But, even then, I knew the satisfaction and fulfillment of being with those people (and eventually convinced the guys to let me shop while they played golf).

There is something about having teammates and dreaming together—figuring out and discerning what God wants to do through us, and sharing the unrelenting commitment to a vision. The striving and struggling, the working side by side to see the vision become a reality. The activity of the mission—even the endless hours and late nights, living passionately, giving our everything. To spend your days knowing people so well you can finish their sentences and bring them their favorite coffee before they even ask for it because you know they need it. A team is a gift.

Who is on your team?

Teachers and Mentors

Ask almost anyone and they can name a favorite teacher from childhood. Teachers do more than give us information; they nurture our intellect, develop skill sets within us, and inspire us to have purpose beyond ourselves. They instill values in us and teach us how to live successfully in many realms of life. Mentors walk beside us, imparting common sense and wisdom almost by osmosis. Through both intentional conversations and things "picked up" along the way, we are made better as people, parents, leaders, and Christ-followers.

My friend Nancy has been a mentor to me. As a young woman in ministry, I faced a leadership crisis early on in my career and wrote her a desperate letter for help. She was kind enough to respond and walk me through it. Little did she know there would be many more phone calls from me needing her insight and wisdom, which she always imparted with such grace. She was and is an example to me of what it means to be a godly woman, a fervent follower of Christ, and a leader of people.

Along with Nancy I have had other mentors and teachers, some with whom I have had a personal relationship and some whom I have never met but have heard them speak or read their books. Some have invested in me personally, and some don't even know they did. Teachers and mentors come in all varieties. We can learn so much from them when our hearts are teachable.

Who is your mentor?

Brothers and Sisters in Christ

The people we truly know in life are ones we see through our eyes and through the eyes of others. I can look at someone and know him or her in a certain way, and you can do the same and it will be a little different. I know my mom, Libby, as my mom. Her brother Albert knows her as a sister. Her friend Marsha knows her as a coworker. If we put our perspectives together, we have a truer understanding of who Libby is.

The same happens in biblical community. I know Jesus in my relationship with him, and my friend Jen knows him in her relationship with him. Of course, our knowledge of him is centered on the Bible, but when she and I share our experiences with Jesus with each other, we know him more and we know him better. There is purpose and power in biblical community, for in it we understand Jesus in deeper ways. When you are part of a community of believers seeking to resemble, serve, and love Jesus, you will get to know him and grow into his likeness.

Biblical community is key to the transformative process not only in us knowing more of Jesus, the one we are seeking to emulate, but also in us understanding what steps we as individuals need to take to be more like him. Brothers and sisters in Christ know each other—we know each other's strengths and weaknesses, gifts and talents. Hopefully our community together is authentic, and we know each other's stories. We know how each of us came to faith in Christ. We know how God has changed each one of us so far, and because of that, we have a vision for each other of who we will be in Christ.

Who are your closest brothers and sisters in Christ right now?

Sacred Places

All through Scripture we read about the places where people encountered God when he showed up in a special or notable way. These places, once ordinary, became known and remembered as holy "spaces." God had been there. Oftentimes, these places were even marked with an altar of some kind, not only in recognition of God's work there, but for the purpose of remembering what he had done: Mt. Moriah, Bethel, Mt. Sinai, Mount of Olives, the upper room, the garden of Gethsemane, the tomb.

God still shows up in places today, encountering people and doing his divine work. We all have places like this. Places that became sacred spaces for us in our faith journey, markers of our own spiritual transformation. And when we remember them, when we think of what God did "there," our faith is built up and strengthened. We are reminded that we can trust him. We are reminded of his great spiritual power in our life. We gain courage and lose fear as we move forward in the next, new thing God is doing in us.

My Sacred Places

There is a retreat center in Western Pennsylvania called Jumonville. On the tippy-top of what are called mountains there (not like the Rockies), is a gigantic cross that can be seen for miles around. In fact, if you climb up there, you can see the landscape of three different states. It was at this retreat center I chose to follow Jesus, and it was at this same place five years later that I surrendered my whole life to him for his use and his glory.

Asilomar was my go-to place in Pacific Grove, California, when I lived in the West. It had once belonged to the YWCA but then became a conference location. If I needed a day of solitude, a weekend of rest, or space to make a decision, I would make the drive. It was this place where God's creation was most beautiful in my eyes and where he spoke to me often. It was here I went to grieve before leaving California. This was where I began writing; it was where I sensed God's presence the strongest.

Hopwood Methodist Church holds a plethora of Christ-filled family memories that shaped me. St. Anthony's in Three Rivers, California is where I first encountered the Stations of the Cross. Sharon Baptist Church in King William, Virginia is where I was baptized and began a vocational career in ministry. My purple chair in the corner of my second-floor studio is a space where God has met me over and over through his Word and prayer.

All of these are sacred places for me.

We all have and need places like this. They are both the markers of God's work in our lives and the places we go when we need him most. We know he has been there; we know he will be there. Sure, God is everywhere, and it's not like these places are particularly Spirit-filled due to their location. But for us they are. They are the handwritten stars on an old-fashioned paper atlas of where we've been and seen him in a significant way, and they are the pop-up location markers on our phone of our favorite spots to meet with him. Some of them are greenhouses for our spiritual formation; some are the butterfly-like "molting" places for us.

Where are your sacred places? Are there places in your life where God really showed up in a significant way? Any places that serve as "markers of faith" for you? Are there spaces that you deem sacred to which you go to spend time with Jesus?

If you are totally new to the journey of faith that I am talking about, it is possible that the place in which you read this book right now may become a sacred place for you. And if you have never considered seeking a space in your home or community where you might go to spend time with Jesus—a place to ask him the most curious questions, to pour out your deepest hurts, to search his Word for the direction you desperately need—you may want to think about that. Sacred places are vital in our spiritual journey. They will be both rest areas and adventure parks, as well as vista points for God's work in you.

Whisper 3: Pay Attention to Where You Are and Who You Are With

I think you get the picture. People matter. Places can have meaning. The people in your life have things to share with you that you need—and vice versa. So don't be a loner. Don't be one of those people who thinks they don't need to "go to church." I understand people don't like "organized religion." But the Bible tells us that the church is people. And since you need people, you need the church. So, I suggest you find one. And as for places, keep your eyes open for the Lord wherever you are. The sacred and the secular are not exclusive of each other. For God, any place and every place is sacred. He is going to show up to meet you in unlikely spaces. Be ready!

WHISPER 4

God Sees You Even If You Can't See Him

Darkness and Doubt

A Different Darkness

When we first moved to Nashville, I spent a lot of time in our home in an overstuffed corner chair by the window watching the birds fly by midair. Months went by. I would read. I would write. But mostly, I would wonder. What new thing did God want me to do in this new place? What was my assignment? My husband's calling was clear, but what about me? There were days when my dreams seemed to be dying; I could not see a future for my life. There were no open doors—and I do mean none, zero, zilch. I was proactive in making contacts and seeking friends, but my efforts yielded no results. Six months turned into one year. After one year, I saw some glimmers of hope, but at eighteen months, still no significant doors opened up. Then came the two-year mark. Let me tell you - that's a lot of bird-watching.

I tried to make the most of all this free time, but the days often felt dark. I had had dark days before, but never a string of several hundred in a row. It was like being in a pitch-black amusement park fun house, and you can't see your hands waving in front of your face, and you don't know where to walk. Or like when the electricity goes off in the house at night and suddenly you can't see to even find a flashlight or candle. It was like being in a movie theater when the screen goes dark to indicate the passing of time in the story, except in my story, the light was not brightening back up. Basically, I just could not see the present or the future, and I began to doubt everything that was in the past. I could not see the light at the end of the tunnel.

And then I realized that I was not actually in a tunnel; there was no need to seek the light at the end. I was shadowed in the Light himself.

In the midst of all this darkness, God was giving me a gift, but I didn't understand it. The darkness he was providing was good, but I didn't see it that way. I mean, darkness is bad, right? Darkness is where fear and confusion make their home and where evil lurks. God is light, and in him there is no darkness, so this can't be good, can it?

That's when I discovered there was a different darkness.

> Those who live in the shelter of the Most High will find rest in the shadow of the Almighty. This I declare about the LORD: He alone is my refuge, my place of safety; he is my God, and I trust him.
>
> (Psalm 91:1–2 NLT)

Up until this point I didn't get it. I thought there was something wrong, when in fact there was something right. I thought this darkness was some kind of punishment, not a kind blessing. I felt afraid, when in fact I was safe. While I could have been resting in his shadow, I was irritated and agitated. This darkness was different than how I usually understood darkness to be. Throwing out all my assumptions about darkness and all my quick categories of how I thought about God, I began to understand that God was revealing himself to me in new ways. I was experiencing God as a shelter, a shadow, and a shield.

A Safe Place

My friend Jenifer has the gift of caution and radar for danger; she is prepared for whatever comes her way. She moved to Tennessee before I did and was well schooled in the threat of tornados. I, on the other hand, did not know that I was moving to "tornado alley." (This is not something they mention in the "C'mon y'all, move to Tennessee" brochures.) Upon my arrival, Jen installed a tornado app on my phone and educated me on the necessity of having a "safe place" in my home. Considering the criteria, the front hall half-bath was chosen. I was ready.

It was in the dead of night when that app exploded in a deafening sound. Disoriented, it took me some time to figure out what was going on. It said I had fifteen minutes to get into my safe place. Dave was out of town, so I was on my own. I could hear the wind howling and whipping around the house. Honestly, I was a little nervous.

I grabbed my phone and burrowed in the hall bathroom. Then I remembered I should have my tablet in there to watch the news. And my phone charger in case this took a while. And a flashlight. And a blanket. And a pillow. And a snack. Maybe a bottle of water.

In and out I went several times as the minutes ticked by until I *had* to be in there.

It was good to know I was safe, but I did feel claustrophobic. I thought about other people in their safe places—many of those in underground spaces. I imagined it being pretty dark for them, and I thought about the real possibility of the electricity going out on me. I was glad I had my flashlight just in case, but still, the thought of being in a small, enclosed, protective space of darkness didn't inspire a sense of safety for me. I was, in fact, afraid in a safe place.

I think it's the same when God shelters us in a storm of life. He provides a safe place for us, hiding us from danger and protecting us from threats. And in that safe place, it can be dark. But it is a different darkness, a good darkness. We don't have to be afraid.

> You hide them in the shelter of your presence, safe from those who conspire against them. You shelter them in your presence far from accusing tongues.
>
> (Psalm 31:20 NLT)

> He will cover you with his feathers. He will shelter you with his wings.
>
> (Psalm 91:4 NLT)

A tornado did touch down that night three miles from our house, destroying the third floor of an apartment building. But no one was hurt. The residents had been where they needed to be: in their safe place.

A Resting Space

It was summer and I was sunbathing. I don't think I had had a tan since I was twentysomething, and now twenty years later, I wasn't working and I had time to spend in the sun. And frankly, now that I wasn't on a church staff, I was doing something I had not done in many years: wearing a bikini. We were living in a new place and I didn't know anyone, so my "free to be me" attitude took over. I felt good and vulnerable all at the same time.

Just as I began to relax a dark shadow suddenly came over me and blocked the sun. I heard a loud *whoosh.* My eyes opened, I jolted up, and there beside me in the backyard was a turkey. Yep.

Turkeys are not your average birds, right? They fly low, you know? The shadow was large and dark! I was feeling vulnerable already and now was fully freaked out. But, I have to say, though startled, the shadow of the turkey did provide relief from the heat. I was afraid of the darkness at first, because I thought I was going to be harmed. But that wasn't the case. Under those wings was a darkness that was cool and welcoming.

> Hide me in the shadow of your wings.
>
> (Psalm 17:8 NLT)

Sometime God casts his presence over us as a shadow, providing a place of rest and bringing relief. We might be afraid at first, but we don't have to be. It is a different darkness—a good darkness.

A Protected Spot

I've seen *Braveheart.* I watched *Gladiator.* I've seen the warriors of times past who carried shields into battle. And I watch the evening news. I've seen the local SWAT team enter real-life, dangerous situations carrying shields for protection. In both cases, as these men and women protected themselves, they had to hold those shields in front of their faces as they moved forward. They had to stand behind them. If they needed to see what was up ahead, they had to peek around the edge. In the darkness behind the shield, they could not see where they were going or what was coming at them, but the shields were necessary for them to remain unharmed.

> But let all who take refuge in you rejoice; let them sing joyful praises forever. Spread your protection over them, that all who love your name may be filled with joy. For you bless the godly, O LORD; you surround them with your shield of love.
>
> (Psalm 5:11–12 NLT)

With God as our shield, as we stand behind him, we may feel like we are in the dark. We may even feel insecure, unsure of what is ahead, when in fact it is the most secure place to be. It is a different darkness, yes, and it is a good darkness.

Discerning the Bad Darkness from the Good Darkness

There is a darkness we all understand—the bad one. We all go through times in our lives that are devastating and tragic, where injustice and evil intent seem to have won. We have times of great loss and grief. There are times when it's not just that things aren't going right, but in fact, everything is going wrong. Problem after problem. Hurt after hurt.

This darkness can't be denied. It is real. But these truly dark seasons don't last forever. Problems do cease. Devastation does stop. Tragedy does become part of the past. But it is my experience that when it seems that the darkness is over and should be lifting, it sticks around. Meaning, there have been so many times when I would see people who had been through something terrible, a dark time in their lives, and when the time came for them to move on, they still felt like they were in a dark place—and they didn't know why. These people would say to me that they felt that God had met them where they needed healing. They felt that they had recovered mostly from the tragic event, even knowing it would always be with them in some way. They now felt a frustration to have the darkness lifted from their lives, but why wasn't it happening?

I never understood this ... until now. I now believe that the darkness that lingers after something terrible happens in our lives is a different darkness. After we have been through something hard, God comes to us seeking to be our shelter and a safe place to be refreshed. He comes to us seeking to cover us with his shadow so that we can sense his presence without interruption or distraction and be renewed. And God comes to us shielding us with his love, protecting us so that we don't have to be afraid as we move forward. This different and good darkness is a place where we get our strength back; it is where relief, redemption, rest, and restoration takes place. This different darkness—it is a gift.

Have you ever experienced the Lord as your shelter, your shadow, or your shield, and you are just realizing it now? I hope you will never look at darkness the same again. I hope you will have eyes to see it when it is good and receive it when it comes to you. I pray all of us would never assume, but seek to discern what we are experiencing—in anything, really. It sounds funny, but what we are asking is that God would give us eyes to see the darkness, and since he is Light, he can do that.

Doubt

I want to talk about *doubt*. A life of genuine growing, transforming faith often includes doubt along the way. It seems contradictory at first, but the fact is a struggle with doubt often precedes a growth in faith. If you don't know this and are intimidated or embarrassed by doubt, you could get stuck in your *becoming*.

My first battle with doubt came when I was still in high school. I had only been a Christian three years or so, and I was struggling with the assurance of my salvation—meaning I just kept wondering if I was really "saved." The Bible is clear that a person only needs to ask Jesus to be his or her Savior once; we don't need to ask over and over again. Once we are his and he is ours, the relationship is eternal. We are his sons and daughters, adopted into the family of God. It is a bond that cannot be broken, even by sin.

Yes, sin can and will hurt the relationship and put a strain on it, but it has no power to break it. The Holy Spirit has put his seal on us. But as a teenager I just could not get my heart to rest in this truth. What if I wasn't really saved? What if I hadn't really asked Jesus into my life? I just delved into introspection and overanalyzed everything. I tried to pick my heart apart, and I did pick my faith apart. I was looking for any impurity that I could find that might impede this decision I had made.

I made myself and my youth leaders crazy. I *needed* an assurance of my salvation. Of course, I had this assurance in God's Word, *and* I proclaimed from my own lips *and* I demonstrated it in my own actions. I ... was ... a ... Christian! Yet, I struggled with doubt. I wanted a document signed by God, hand-delivered by an angel. I needed to see some heavyweight paper, written in black ink, with a signature from God's own calligraphy pen, in the mailbox. I realize now that these were the beginnings of understanding and having faith. But at the time, it was just so hard to grasp.

The good news was I wanted the right thing, and I was pursuing the right One. My leaders continued to teach me God's Word in the midst of my doubtful feelings. And though I believe this is something many people go through, I do wish that I had not tried so hard. All that overthinking of faith was exhausting to the new believer that I was—and it wasn't necessary. God wasn't the one rushing me to certainty in my beliefs; I was doing that all by myself.

So, if you find yourself struggling with doubt early on in your faith, I suggest you be patient with yourself. Don't let your feelings and questions drive the day. Simply keep reading your Bible, hang out with people who can teach you God's ways, obey what you know each day, and just allow your faith to be nurtured that it may grow.

My second battle with doubt (and for me, more challenging than the first) was in college. There I was in the middle of learning about and practicing ministry: I was leading, teaching, and serving diligently ... and I doubted everything. Was God real? Was Jesus really God? Was sin a real thing? Was the cross a real deal? Did I really need to be saved? Did God *really* know my name? I mean, I was a mess, really.

At that point I had staked eight years of my life already on this Christian "thing," and now I wasn't sure. And I was scared, to be honest with you. So, I went back to the beginning. I researched my faith all over again. I went back to a few "square one" type things that I had not done at the age of thirteen. I took a second look at the Bible and its validity. I revisited the life of Jesus in history. I rethought the "why" and meaning and work of faith as a follower of Jesus. I read about the reason and role of suffering in the world. In other words, I got my brain in on my faith more than I had earlier.

And then, I reengaged my heart with the God who had been with me in his very presence so many times. I reflected on the ways he had comforted me and led me through sorrows and challenges. I thanked him for the joys and blessings that had come from him. And then, probably the most important thing I did was talk to a few close friends. I did not run and hide. I did step back from a few ministry tasks/responsibilities, but *I stayed* with my brothers and sisters in Christ. We talked, and they were there for me as I went through it all.

Someone suggested I read a book by a Campus Crusade staffer at the time, Jackie Hudson, called *Doubt: A Road to Growth*. Doubt, when addressed in the Bible, is always about moving from doubt toward faith. I noted in the book, "I am grateful for my time of darkness. Doubt was a good teacher, for out of it came one of the most valuable lessons I have learned in life: People grow better in grace."[6]

The things she said were true. My self-effort and self-sufficiency waned in the face of doubt—and that was a good thing. When I doubted, my self-reliance went away; my focus moved more toward Jesus. I became less judgmental of others who struggled with matters of faith, because now I knew what that was like. I was not interested in the "rules" of God or any sort of legalism; plain and simple, I needed him.

Since then, though less dramatic, I have had more times of doubt in my life. Frankly, doubts come. They are part of being human and part of living by faith. Doubt is not wrong nor is it something to be embarrassed about. It does not have to cripple you, and it does not have to scare you. When doubt comes, the best thing we can do is acknowledge it and let it fuel our growth toward a stronger faith.

Whisper 4: God Sees You Even If You Can't See Him

There will be times in your ever-changing life when you feel you just can't see God. Life will seem dark and God not present; doubts will rise up as faith seems to dwindle. There you will be, seeking to be transformed into his likeness, and you will feel like he has disappeared. As a result, you will start to wonder if he cares about you at all. Don't panic. When this happens, you are going to have to dig deep and let your faith grow. The unrest and distrust is indeed only a feeling. He *is* with you. He *has not* forgotten you. He *does care* about you. He ... sees ... you.

Whisper 5

He Knows You Better Than You Know Yourself

Beloved and True

Beloved

I remember we went to a church where the pastor always addressed the congregation as "Beloved." I didn't like it. It sounded traditional or something. And something about it felt fake to me. I knew the Bible referred to God's people as "beloved," but it just didn't have much meaning for me. I'm sure I rolled my eyes more than once. I knew I was one of God's people, and I didn't need to be called "beloved."

In later years there was a time in my life when I doubted God's love for me. I was hitting dead ends relationally, professionally, and spiritually, and I sensed I was surrounded by a "spirit of rejection." I am not trying to be hyperreligious, but I want you to understand I do mean a spirit of rejection. It was a spiritual warfare, wrestling match event in my life, and the Evil One was throwing down hard. I kept praying and seeking to end the battle; I was committed to acting in faith. When I saw a possible relational connection, I followed it up. When what seemed like a professional opportunity came my way, I followed it through. When God revealed a spiritual truth to me, I wrote it down. But still no change; I was losing the fight.

On my bookshelf was *Life of the Beloved* by Henri Nouwen. I think I read it in seminary, but now I reached for it in desperation. Though I could not remember the content of the book, the word *beloved* was drawing me in. There in those pages, Henri introduced me to something I had never heard of: self-rejection. He said the greatest trap in our lives is not success, popularity, or power, but self-rejection. Self-rejection has us believing we need to do something relevant, spectacular, or powerful to be worth loving. Self-rejection internalizes every accusation, criticism, abandonment, and rejection. Self-rejection says, "I am no good … I deserve to be pushed aside, forgotten, rejected …"

The bulb in my head switched on.

> Self-Rejection is the greatest enemy of the spiritual life because it contradicts the sacred voice that calls us the Beloved. Being the Beloved expresses the core truth of our existence.[7]

My eyes squinted at the bright light of truth revealed. The spirit of rejection I was truly struggling with was within. And I was spinning my wheels on the outside trying to make it go away. I kept thinking if I prepared more and equipped myself better; if I served harder and believed "bigger," then surely I would become all that God wanted me to be—or what I *thought* he wanted me to be.

Chosen

When I was in school, I did not like gym class. I was not athletic and everyone knew it. I had friends in class, but when it came time to pick teams, even my friends left me high and dry. I was always near last to be picked. Over those years, there were many gym classes in which to be passed over. Not chosen.

In high school, I was a high honor student and part of the NHS, National Honor Society. You would think I would have been happy with that, but instead I lived with the nagging disappointment that I had not been chosen for GATE, the Gifted and Talented Education program. Good grades? Yes. Hard worker? Yes. Gifted and talented? No. Not chosen.

In my senior year of high school, I ran for class president. Though I was not popular, I was somewhat respected and had already served as treasurer and vice president. I had planned our prom and other events and was excited by the idea that I would plan our class reunions, etc., for years to come. The girl who ran against me was not a leader type, but a very pretty girl with a more popular reputation. I lost. She won. Once again, not chosen.

Can you imagine that nearly thirty years later I still remember these things? And this is not to say that I haven't ever experienced being "chosen." I have been chosen for many things. But it is the not-chosen moments that resonate the loudest. It shouldn't be this way and is evidence of how misdirected our minds and hearts can be. For me, it is a fight to keep my focus on who God has made me to be rather than wishing to be somebody or something else. It is hard to get it through my thick skull that God has chosen me. I think this is because other people's lives appear to be "more chosen" than mine.

Nouwen speaks about how we think that if someone is chosen, then that means someone else is not chosen. Like, where there is a winner, there is a loser. Yet, God's kingdom does not work this way. His heart is not like this. God is deeply in love with all people—every single one of us. His heart is big enough for the volume of hearts he creates. We are each uniquely designed with being and purpose. What everyone else is being and doing does not have an impact on us. We are still who we are created to be and do. And we bring that to the community of God's people and to the world without any slant or pushing in from other people's design.

But that doesn't seem real to me. It is so incongruent with how the world works that I can't get my brain wrapped around it. In the world where I live, our being and purpose is evaluated every day and judged, and depending on how good you really are at something or how popular you rise to be, this determines your success in life and the extent of influence you will have. It is up to you to make it happen and to try to get out there in front of people so they will choose you.

Even inside the church, we acknowledge that God lifts certain people up to have a great influence among their generation, etc. Well, I aspire to that ... I want to do that ... how do you get chosen for that? So you keep trying to make your way and earn a spot. The next thing you know you find yourself trying to earn your way with God and wondering why he didn't pick you for the "A" team.

It's like being in high school all over again. We all want to be part of the "in" group. We all want to be "cool." We all want to be recognized as being at the top of our game. So no matter where you work, as a believer this is all something to be reckoned with inside of yourself. Being chosen for God's "A" team happened the day you committed your life to following him. The day you became born-again is the day he was waiting and hoping for. When he created you, he already chose you. He's been waiting for you to choose him.

It is hard to convince oneself that you are the beloved, and I don't know if there is a way to proceed in doing so. I keep hoping for a breakthrough moment when I will finally get it, believe it, and live in it. And sometimes I fear that moment is not going to come. What if, for whatever reason, I am stuck and won't ever truly understand who I am in Christ? When I consider this possibility, fear rises up in me. I am afraid I am going to mess this up—this gift of the Christian life that God has freely given. What if I squander it as a result of lack of understanding?

When I think these thoughts, I have to slow down the panic in my mind and place my focus back on Christ, for this is not something I have to figure out and seek to attain. Being the beloved is already who I am. My only part in this is to follow Christ as he leads me and transforms me into who he has made me to be—already.

And so, what would it look like if we believed we were chosen and invited to live as the beloved? I think we would love God with all our hearts and minds and souls. We would love ourselves and love others. If we lived as the beloved, we would possess the needed self-confidence to fulfill our purpose on earth and not be discouraged by someone else's success. Why? Because we would know that with God, *we will* fulfill our unique calling. No doubt about it. Our eyes on him, our feet following his, our souls empowered by his Spirit, and with him as our first love, there are no obstacles that cannot be crossed and no mistakes or misdirection that will not be redeemed and reset for our best and his glory.

> Put on then, as God's chosen ones, holy and beloved, compassionate hearts, kindness, humility, meekness, and patience.
>
> (Colossians 3:12 ESV)

My True Self

"Be true to yourself," people say. I don't know if that is the same as being your true self. Mostly I am not a person who gives in to peer pressure. I stick to my convictions, and most often my final decision aligns with who I am. However, the road getting there is not easy; the process wears on me. Why? Because I still have people-pleasing tendencies. Yes, I want people to like me. Yes, I want people to be happy.

I've read the books on boundaries. I've read books on approval addiction. I've attended sessions on dealing with criticism. I've prayed for years to have a thicker skin, but it never came to be. And though I maintained my strength in making final decisions regarding life matters, I always struggled with the pressure in that process pushing in on my core identity, fueling insecurity and creating self-doubt that was emotionally paralyzing. Yes, in faith, with God's help, I made good decisions, but I could not get over the nagging sense that something was not right. Peace eluded me even though I had "done the right thing." A sense of unrest nagged at me. Constantly.

It was this unexplainable unrest within me that drove me to search for what I now acknowledge as my "true self." I didn't always know there was a true self and a false self. Counselors know this. Psychologists know this. Some people just live it without having to think about it. But, not me. I didn't know it, and I did need to think about it.

So, I sat down and did a self-evaluation. I reviewed the multiple personality tests I had taken over the years (um, to be clear ... I'm talking about multiple *tests* on personality). I reviewed my talents and spiritual gift assessments. I combed through some of my journals. I took a hard look at how I spend my time and treasure. I checked in to see if my passions had changed. I reviewed and revised my personal mission statement.

This seemed like such a good idea. But the fact is, it really didn't help me. I did not feel better. The unexplainable unrest remained unclear.

Then I realized I had made a mistake. I was trying to solve the problem the wrong way. It was pastor and author Eugene Peterson who got me back on track. In his book *Run with the Horses* he says, "My identity does not begin when I begin to understand myself. There is something previous to what I think about myself, and it is what God thinks of me.[8]

Ugh. I had started with me. I should have started with God. (Herein lies a mistake I've made more often than I am aware of.) So, after this revelation, I searched out my unrest differently and discovered what I really needed to know. Here is what I learned.

The False Self

Basically, the false self is defined by what I have, what I can do, and what others think of me. So, in order to have my "best" false self, I am constantly gathering possessions of all kinds, doing all I can do every minute of the day, and being motivated by the approval of others in hopes I will feel good about who I am. If I can acquire more and more of the right things, then maybe I can be "full." If I can work hard enough, be successful enough, be important enough, then maybe I will be "complete." If I can gain a roster of accolades, a following of fans, the constant approval of others, then hopefully I will be "happy."

The problem is, the false self is insatiable. I will never have enough stuff, never be successful enough, and never earn enough approval for my false self to rest its agenda. The false self has no mercy, and it is loveless.

The True Self

My true self, on the other hand, is defined by my Creator, God. When our life is based in him we find the deepest fulfillment. David Benner, in his book *The Gift of Being Yourself*, talks about what it is like to find your true self:

> It is like putting on a perfectly custom-tailored dress or suit after wearing clothes made for other people. Our self-in-Christ is a self that fits perfectly because it is completely us. It is a self that allows us to be free of all anxiety regarding how we should be and who we are. And it allows us to be absolutely our self- unique not by virtue of our strivings for individuality but profoundly original simply because that is who and what we are. God's call to our fulfillment is therefore a call to take our place in his grand restoration agenda of making all things new in Christ.[9]

My ... soul ... breathed.

> "For you died to this life, and your real life is hidden with Christ in God"
>
> (Colossians 3:3 NLT).

That was it. This is what I wanted: my real life in Christ. I wanted to be myself as he had made me to be. No wishing to be someone else. No striving for things intended to be out of my reach. No anxiety about not living up to expectations. No more breathless chasing after elusive perfection.

Benner says that our calling in life will be both best for us and best for the world, and we will live it out in dependence on the will of God. That's what I have always wanted, and in many ways I did exactly this. But I misstepped along the way, too. I have cared about what others thought about me a great deal and let their expectations shape me too much. No doubt, I have been more self-reliant than God-reliant many a day.

The Process Is a Pursuit

I can tell you that the process of discovering one's true self can be a lifelong journey. It doesn't have to be, but it could be. So much of it depends on your life experiences, how much of the world's weak wisdom you have taken into your heart, and how diligent you are in your part of your spiritual formation. The examination of one's heart can be hard work. You have to be vulnerable.

When you find something inside yourself that you are not proud of or that you are embarrassed of, you can't just hide it again and hope God didn't see it when you did. You have to bring it out into his light so that, together, you can decide what to do with it. You already know that trials and challenges often reveal who we really are. Under too much pressure, whatever is under the surface of our skin seeps out, and if it's not good, well now, everyone knows it. We try, then, to avoid situations where the heat is turned up in our lives. We avoid conflict. We avoid pain. We would rather ignore the negative things we feel than acknowledge them and seek out their origin. Thomas Merton wisely admonishes us with this:

> Therefore if you spend your life trying to escape from the heat of the fire that is meant to soften and prepare you to become your true self, and if you try to keep your substance from melting in the fire—as if your true identity were to be hard wax—the seal will fall upon you at last and crush you. You will not be able to take your own true name and countenance, and you will be destroyed by the event that was meant to be your fulfillment.[10]

See, when God created the world, he did not intend for his creation to suffer, but the free will of humankind has led us down wretched roads. Yet, God redeems our circumstances. He redeems the hurts we experience. Events that are painful or even tragic are the very things that God uses in our lives to get rid of that which is ill-advised and not important so that our lives in him can be revealed. Surrender runs *toward* God in these times, not away from him. Rather than avoid, we need to engage. Why? So that we can be freely and truly ourselves.

But it's not just in the harder times of life we learn to lean into our true selves. In the culture we live in, it would be best to intentionally engage in understanding and expressing "our hidden life in Christ." I realize all of this sounds like hard work. Frankly, any pursuit takes some effort. But I hope you understand that it is not work in the sense that the results are dependent on us. This is not about us being smart or wise or making this happen.

God is the one with all the knowledge and know-how. He leads us to our true selves. David Benner says that it is in first knowing the I AM, God himself, that we will then come to know "I," meaning, "myself." God already knows who we are, and he guides us to discover the truth. Our part in the process is to surrender and to be obedient. I believe most Christians trust God enough to surrender, and they want to say yes to what God has for them. The hardest part, really, is in saying no and the letting go. We have to let go of the old life—the life before we knew Christ—so that we can see who we are now; so we can get a glimpse of who we are becoming.

And So Now

Here it is in a nutshell. When I came to Christ, I died to my life that was informed by the world's ways and values; I died to a mistaken understanding of my "self." In finding Christ, I found my true life. I found the true understanding of my "self" as defined by God. It is a daily vigil to live from my true self that is hidden in God. Little by little I let go of the old ways I defined myself, and I embrace the truth of who I am in Christ. I make constant decisions to let go of people-pleasing and approval-seeking.

Fear of criticism no longer debilitates me, and practicing boundaries does not take all my emotional resources. God knows me and makes a way for me. I know him and I make my way through him. It's not easy, but it's easier. It is not always peaceful, but it is peace-filled. The soul doesn't sleep, but it does rest; and it rests deeply.

> To work out our own identity in God ... is a labor that requires sacrifice and anguish, risk and many tears. It demands close attention to reality at every moment, and great fidelity to God as He reveals Himself, obscurely, in the mystery of each new situation. We do not know clearly beforehand what the result of this work will be. The secret of my full identity is hidden in Him. He alone can make me who I am, or rather who I will be when at last I fully begin to be ...

> The way of doing it is a secret I can learn from no one else but Him. There is no way of attaining to the secret without faith ... The secret of my identity is hidden in the love and mercy of God.[11]

Whisper 5: He Knows You Better Than You Know Yourself

Maybe you are a person who has been blessed with a natural, healthy self-awareness and self-understanding. God knows you, and you know you, and you are good with all that. But for many people, myself included, we need reminding that God knows us inside and out, through and through. And we need reminding that though there are days we are unsure of ourselves, unsure of our emotions, and unsure of who we really are, we can still trust God. His knowledge of us and his love are unwavering. There is no better one to guide us through a soul metamorphosis than the soul maker himself.

> Beloved, we are God's children now, and what we will be has not yet appeared; but we know that when he appears we shall be like him, because we shall see him as he is.
>
> (1 John 3:2 ESV)

WHISPER 6

Take a Step

Sin and Struggles

Umm ... Sin

Sin is not a popular topic. Really, no one likes to talk about it. And because of that, I think that it is often misunderstood. Usually when people think of sin, they think of a list of really bad behaviors. While this list is probably not wrong, it does not tell the whole story. Sin is a condition before it is an action. Humankind, while wonderfully created in the image of God, is also born sinful. And while we could sit around and blame Adam and Eve, it's not like we don't know our own wayward hearts and the choices we have made. We have all been selfish, turning away from God at one point or another. Aware of his perfection and holiness, we are certain that we are neither—and surprisingly, nor do we have to be. See, Jesus is the friend of sinners. He is not the kind of person to shy away from someone who is in the wrong, doing wrong, or planning on wrongdoing. In fact, he pursues those people—and by "those people," I mean "us."

Jesus is a friend of sinners. The historical account of his life demonstrates this. One after another he pursues and receives people whom others have discarded. The forgotten, the forlorn, the villain, the victim, the outcast, and the outlaw—he is their friend. He does not shy away from those who don't know him or are against him; he is not put off. He loves people unconditionally and completely and is more concerned about where they are going than where they have been. And for all of us, in the moments when we understand that we have walked away from him, our hearts broken and repentant, longing to be forgiven and to follow him, we find he is there with open arms and open hands. Jesus urges and ushers us back to himself.

In light of this, we need not be torn or derailed in our relationship with God by our struggle with sin. He knows and understands who we are and where we live, and he knows where we are headed. He does not shame us or condemn us. His heart is for us not against us. His love is everlasting, and his patience does not wear out.

In trusting him as Savior, he sees us forgiven. We have his Spirit within us, and with that come spiritual eyes to see life *as he sees it* and a power to overcome anything we need to. He is *for us* all the way and always. So don't allow sin and struggles to paralyze you in your faith journey. His presence and power are yours for this time and place, this situation and that circumstance. He will provide whatever you need to walk away from sin and toward him, but you will need to actually take a step.

Sin Gets in the Way

We could say that sin impedes, inhibits, hinders, hampers, obstructs, foils, ruins, shackles, delays, threatens, and thwarts the changes that God is making in your life. But I think we will just plainly say it.

Sin gets in the way.

If we desire to be transformed by God into his likeness—a living testament of his love, kindness, mercy, and more—then we have to contend with sin as a real threat and deal with it as such. Galatians 5:19–21 says this:

> The acts of the sinful nature are obvious: sexual immorality, impurity and debauchery; idolatry and witchcraft; hatred, discord, jealousy, fits of rage, selfish ambition, dissensions, factions, and envy; drunkenness, orgies, and the like.
>
> (NIV)

Most of those, as stated, are probably obvious. But, maybe not all. If I had made a list in my own mind, I don't know if I would have thought to include discord, jealousy, and selfish ambition. Those just seem like run-of-the mill, everyday human issues. But they're not. A step toward discord is a step away from unity. A step toward jealousy is a step away from contentment. A step toward selfish ambition is a step away from God's plan. And the fact is, unity, contentment, and God's plan all matter to what he is accomplishing in each of us. Those things can't be compromised.

Can you hear what I am saying? Sin is a big problem in every which way—eternally and currently in your life. Jesus gave his life to erase the eternal consequence of it, and he lives inside you now to empower you away from it. Sin does not care about you; it does not have your best interest at heart, and no matter how it good it claims to be, there is nothing good about it. It makes promises that it will never deliver. It lies and cheats and deceives.

Dissatisfaction, disaster, and disappointment—that is what it is about. Do not let it become a burden to your soul; do not let it slow you down in your faith journey. Every step you take in life needs to be toward Jesus. Period. Not toward anything else.

Secrets

One of the big mistakes I made in life regarded a dating relationship I had. I dated a Christian guy who was in ministry leadership alongside me. Committed to the same things in life, he seemed perfect for me. It was recommended that leaders not date each other for the sake of team unity and focus, so we kept our relationship a secret. Not even my roommate knew about it. Little by little, things moved toward a sensual focus, and my morals and self-respect slipped away.

Though we never actually went "all the way," to this day my mind has blocked out some of what happened between us physically. I thought I was preserving my purity by not taking that last step, and I remain glad that I didn't. But, our relationship was still very unhealthy and frankly, toxic; he was a master manipulator. I didn't know that then, but I knew it much later. The fact is that if I had been in a healthy relationship, I would have been discussing it with my girlfriends as girls do, and if not I, then they would have seen the red flags of how wrong this was. But because of my secret, I had stopped cultivating transparency in all my relationships and was compromised in so many ways.

Sadly, the truth is that I was not the one who ended it. He did. He found another girl, a sister in Christ, a friend, and he began a public relationship with her. And when I confronted him about it, he told everyone I was lying about our relationship and making the whole thing up. It was a terrible time of my life, and it was years before people found out the truth about him.

It is not my fault that this is who he was. But I kept a secret that made me vulnerable. I hid the truth because I knew it was wrong, but I wanted it anyways. I was irresponsible with my own life. That's on me. I was on the road away from Christlikeness. Yet, God did as he always does. When my sin was brought out into the light, he redeemed it and restored me. In my own hands, the situation was destructive; in his hands it was something used to shape me and build me up with grace and mercy.

Are there any sinful behaviors you are dealing with in your life right now? Do you have any secrets?

Temptation

In this life there are temptations. Satan (the Evil One, the Devil, the Prince of Darkness—whatever you want to call him) is always throwing things at people in an effort to draw them away from the Lord. He will do anything to keep you from becoming who God plans for you to be.

Temptation can seem harmless at times, but it is actually dangerous. While it is not a sin in and of itself, it does lead to sin. Walking along beside a temptation can seem like *no big deal*, but the next thing you know, you may find yourself stopped and standing there with it—just hanging out with temptation as if it is a friend. And then you might begin to give it some attention, and before you know it, what you once would never *consider* you are now *considering*. The next thing you know, you find yourself sitting down with what was once only temptation and is now actually sin, and you are immersed in it. You really did not think you would end up "here," you say to yourself. Now, you have *a big deal* on your hands.

Right from the beginning, the key to undermining temptation is to make corrections in your thinking, in smaller increments, so that you will not have to later make any major adjustments that might be painful. It is said, "The pain of discipline costs far less than the pain of regret." When you are tempted, don't nurture that temptation! When your mind wanders to sin, put your focus back on God. Desire will become action, so we best set our desires on the right and good things of God. So, when you take a step, make sure it is toward God and away from temptation.

The Ant Trail

One day my husband and I woke up to find an ant trail in our bathroom. A hundred or more ants were marching into the lower cabinet. Opening the door, we found the parade destination: a box of sweet cherry cough drops. The ants had found an opening on one side of the box and were clamoring to get what they thought was a sweet treat. Interestingly enough, on the opposite side of the box the ants had found an exit. A second ant trail was proceeding *away* from the box, and boy, did it look different. There was no anticipation of a sugar high for these ants. They were clearly sluggish, and many of them were dying in their tracks. See, the active ingredient in the cough drops was killing them. What had looked so good, in fact, was not good at all.

Get it? There will always be temptations like sweet cherry cough drops presenting themselves as attractive, delicious opportunities for our lives. But, they are not what they seem. Wrapped inside is something harmful to the soul.

Have you encountered any of those in your own life path of recent? Turn around and walk the other way!

Watch and Pray, Crucify and Choose

I sometimes ask myself, How will I have the willpower to withstand the temptation of sin as long as I live? ... and then I have to remind myself that it is not about *my* power at all. It is about God's power in me. What I need to do is watch and pray. I need to be on the lookout for evil that comes my way. It is for me to be alert, not asleep at the wheel. I need to be with other Christ-followers who watch with me and for me while I watch with and for them, and we encourage one another.

And then I need to pray. Not only asking God for his direction in my life, but praying his truth for my life. It is the Word of God that will strengthen me against sin. So I read it. I pray it. This I can do. And once I do that, I can do anything. I watch and pray for the day that I will see Jesus face-to-face. I keep in mind that he is with me and he is coming back. I seek to live according to the new life I have in the Spirit (Galatians 5:16), meaning that I seek to "go on living" according to the Spirit. It is an ongoing thing, not a one-time thing. I must continually, actively listen and obey the Holy Spirit. The Christian life is not one of rote behaviors; it is an organic, mystery-filled adventure of movement. And within this animated life of movement and mystery, there are two things that set down the tracks for staying on course with God.

1. Crucify the sin.

> Those who belong to Christ Jesus have nailed the passions and desires of their sinful nature to his cross and crucified them there.
>
> (Galatians 5:24 NLT)

2. Choose the Spirit.

> Since we are living by the Spirit, let us follow the Spirit's leading in every part of our lives.
>
> (Galatians 5:25 NLT)

There's no mystery about these two things. You gotta do the first one. And you gotta do the second one. Always. One after the other, and over again as needed. These two practical applications of Scripture in our lives will keep us in the flow of the Spirit.

Run *Your* Race

The Bible says, "Therefore, since we are surrounded by such a great cloud of witnesses, let us throw off everything that hinders and the sin that so easily entangles, and let us run with perseverance the race marked out for us" (Hebrews 12:1 NIV). I believe if you take steps like we have been talking about, soon you will be running. You remember when your child took his or her first step? Next thing you knew, they were gallivanting around the house!

Thus, the direction of your steps matter. Taking a step toward Jesus means that you will soon be running toward him. If you take a step away from Jesus, soon you may find yourself running away from him. I don't want that for you. Running *away* from temptation and sin and running *to* Jesus is the best kind of race. And, it has the biggest prize.

My husband is a seven-time Ironman. After swimming, biking, and running 140.6 miles on a given day with 2,300 other people, he runs across the line marking a race finish. In the early morning as the event is set to begin, there is a phrase you will hear the participants say to themselves and to each other: "Keep your focus and run *your* race."

They say this because they know it is not about how someone else would do it; this race is yours and you have to run it how you want to run it. You have prepared and you have planned for it. You have unique strengths and weaknesses that you will navigate along the way. You will have transitions that are yours to maximize for your best race. It is not about someone else's nutrition, technique, or mind-set. It is about you and how you are going to get across that finish line. Each racer has his own race to run and his own way of getting it done. And I would say that the Christian *race* that apostle Paul talks about in Hebrews is no different.

The Church is made up of believers who are following Christ, running a race with their eyes on the prize of eternal life. From Scripture we know that yes, we are running it together, relying on each other for encouragement. And yes, the victory will be one we share. But, each of us is running a race that is uniquely ours and significantly designed and coached by God. And while we can learn from each other, we are not to compare our races. You don't need to feel the pressure of doing it like someone else. Your race is a unique expression of Jesus in you that is not to be shadowed or copied. Your Christian life is distinctly you and Jesus: no one else can match it. So, keep your eyes on him and run strong.

Run *your* race.

Struggles of Every Kind

Life on earth as a human has struggles. No perfect pedigree, outrageous riches, or cushy circumstances can alter that fact. Heartaches and disappointments will always come.

One of the most universal and challenging struggles we will ever face is the healing of a wounded heart. An emotional hurt cuts deep and can hinder our growth as a person; a laceration of the soul can quickly cut off the flow of transformation in our life.

When we find ourselves in a situation like this, we cannot sit around waiting for someone else to take the first step. We need to take a step. We need to initiate the healing process. And that means stepping out and stepping up to either talk directly with the person who hurt us or decide to get whatever help *we* need. If you felt physically sick, you would go to the doctor. If you had a physical injury, you would rush to the emergency room. And so it is with emotional pain. We need to do something about it rather than ignore it.

So often we hesitate to act. We don't ask for help. Instead, we cocoon; we hide from God and others because we are afraid. Afraid the wound is too deep; afraid the healing process will only bring more pain. We wonder what will be required of us in the process, and we are angry that we have to go through this. The path of least resistance is to ignore the whole ordeal and nurse the wound privately. So, that is what we often do. And if we choose that course, then our ever-changing lives stop moving forward. We get stuck. Metamorphosis interrupted.

I'm sure you can guess that this is not what God wants for you. God wants you to initiate the healing process by opening up to him. God is the one who is the Great Physician. He is the healer of hearts and souls. The Bible says that he is the one who heals the brokenhearted and bandages their wounds (Psalm 147:3 NLT). In our trouble, we can cry out to him. He will comfort us and ultimately make us whole.

If you are crippled by a wounded heart turn to God and do this: first, cleanse the wound with the living water, meaning, talk it out with Jesus. Let him cleanse it of any impurities that are there. If you have any fault in the acquiring of this wound, confess it. Second, apply the healing balm of the Word, meaning, read the Word. Search the Bible for the Scriptures that speak to your situation. Say them out loud. Put them on Post-it notes anywhere you will be all day long. Memorize them. Third, cover the wound with prayer. Prayer will guard it from being injured further as well as release God's power to work in the healing process. Ask God to give you what you need for healing (understanding, release, love, courage, etc.).

When the time is right, consider it healed and "take off the bandage." Let the healed wound breathe. What that really means is that you will need to be vulnerable again. Up until now you have nursed the wound, and that is okay for a time, but now you are ready to live again, risking if necessary. You are ready for new relationships, ready for new adventures. You are ready for whatever is next. Soon you will find that the healing of this wound is now part of your transformational story. By surrendering your struggle to the Lord, you gave him permission to use it in your life and he did. Now, you are different. You are changed for the better. Your faith is stronger. Your heart is more like his.

Any struggle you are facing, any wound of the heart can be redeemed for good in your life. Is there a step toward healing that you need to take today?

Whisper 6: Take a Step

Remember what we said? Jesus is a friend of sinners. He understands our struggles, and he makes a way for us to take a step toward him every single time. The Bible says, "If we confess our sins, he is faithful and just and will forgive us our sins and purify us from all unrighteousness" (1 John 1:9 NIV). There is not enough willpower to bulldoze sin out of our life. Confession is what is needed – and then Jesus gets sin out of the way for us. And then, when we take a step toward what he is doing in our lives, we will begin to see the fruit of the Spirit birthed and formed in our souls. God will shape and mold us into people of love, joy, peace, patience, kindness, goodness, faithfulness, gentleness, and self-control. And as these things are manifested in us, they will overflow; our transformation, then, will begin to take flight, and our lives will make a difference in the world. You don't want to miss that. Take ... a ... step.

WHISPER 7

You Are a Unique Contribution to the World

Being and Doing

Layers

Layers have a good reputation in the culinary world. Like lasagna. Like that big chocolate truffle cake people make in a clear glass bowl. Or seven-layer salad (where mayo is an entire layer!). And, of course, the famous layered taco dip. Then there are layers as related to fashion, which is fun (if you're into that).

Layers are rich whether you are eating them or wearing them. But the richest layers I have ever seen are those that make up the Grand Canyon. Creationist or evolutionist, it doesn't matter: the Grand Canyon is a sight to be reckoned with. Those layers are mesmerizing, right? All those horizontal lines of shaded earth tones! I could sit and stare for hours.

And then there are the layers underneath my skin, the layers that I am made of.

As humans we have layers of personality, experience, and emotions. My soul has lots of layers. Sometimes it is said that we are like an onion, and we need to peel away the layers and understand them. As a result, we will be rewarded by getting to the core of who we are (and maybe what is really bothering us). I don't disagree with this process, and it is important to know ourselves and get to the core of our issues, etc., but I think the Grand Canyon reveals something more important to keep in mind: there is beauty in the layers.

Every layer has worth and its own meaning. Every layer is what makes me, me. If I isolated one layer that had the coarsest texture and lusterless color, it would probably look awful. And actually, in the light it might look even worse than awful. But when I put all the layers together, well, it is a bit breathtaking. The layers of my life tell my story.

The best pictures of the Grand Canyon are those taken when sunlight is moving across it. The angles and movement of the light change how it all looks. It is spectacular! Not trying to overspiritualize, but in our own lives I can see how the light of Christ shining on and through us makes us look different. All of the nuances and essences, all the shades and details his light exposes and highlights show that we are wonderfully alive and woven together.

For you see, what Christ does in your life is the real wonder of the world. When you take time to see the result of his transforming work in you, no doubt you will then be ready and willing to move forward in faith, trusting God with the next layer that's in the making. God is doing something special in you. And I don't say *special* like there are pink ponies and rainbow stars circling your head. I mean this: you are a unique contribution to the world.

Watching the Watch

So often we want to *do* in order to *be*. We think if we feel good about our *doing* then we will feel good about our *being*. If my work is worthy, then I will be worthy. If I perform well and impress others, that means I am somebody and I matter. We begin to depend on the results of our work to give us true fulfillment. Our *being* becomes reliant on our *doing*.

Consequently, too often we do things to gain our identity by role, position, or promotion. We try to earn our way into relationships rather than seek authentic connection. We unconsciously create a wall of flurried activity to mask our insecurities, thinking that the more we do, the less guilt we will feel. Often, we keep our noses to the grindstone with shame as our motivation.

Every personality test I have ever taken has shown me to be a type A overachiever with "striving" as a strength. And being one who internally linked my accomplishments to my identity, I tried to accomplish everything possible, at the highest level—every day. To do this, I trained myself to make the best use of the clock. I was always asking myself, how can I get more done in less time? I was committed that every moment of my day would have purpose so that my life would count for something.

I used to be a leader in programming: I directed events and told everyone where to go, when to walk, what to do, and I was the timekeeper. So naturally, when my friend Jen got married I helped with the flow of the service. Later, I saw a picture from the wedding. It was intended to feature a behind-the-scenes shot with the bride. In that pic, in the background, there I was looking at my watch. Now of course, I was in charge of watching the time, so that should be no surprise. But when I saw that picture, I realized that if someone snapped a shot of me on any given day at any time, I would probably be watching my watch. I was always watching my watch! I feared that if everything wasn't timed just right, I would fail. More than that, I knew I had an inner fear that if I wasn't *doing* and accomplishing all the time, I was somehow going to miss out on all that God was making me *to be*.

Something clicked that day and I decided I didn't want to watch my watch anymore. So I took it off. After that, I never wore a watch on a regular basis, only on occasion when needed. Truth be told, no one needs a watch all the time. We don't have to know what time it is every moment. We don't have to be aware of every passing minute. I know we are afraid time will get away from us, whether it is the time in a single day or the kind of long-term time when your kids grow up and you feel like you missed it. I understand this. But that will solve itself if we will simply be focused on the present.

It is actually living in the present that makes sure we won't miss anything in the future. We don't have to depend on the clock. The two hands on the clock are not to be the primary directors of the day; our two hands need to be. We need to be feeling and touching and experiencing life right now. When we do that, we are in the flow of how God is using the time of our lives as a transforming agent. So, take off the watch and let God handle your time. *Let him do* what he wants to do so that *you can be.*

Time Change

My husband says that daylight savings weekend is his favorite "holiday." He celebrates the night when he gets an extra hour of sleep. It is a time change he appreciates that one night! Most people, though, like when the time changes in the Spring – more sunlight in the evenings!

You have turned your clock back one hour and forward one hour many times and you already know this: a time change makes a difference.

And a time change in our lives is often what we need.

I was in college when I first heard the term *hurry-sickness*, and I knew that I had it. I was always rushed. I had a *list* of to-do *lists* that never got done. I always felt behind, and I felt guilty if I relaxed. I wish I could say that I figured out in college how to tame the monster of busyness, but I did not. In fact, throughout most of my adult life, I mistook busyness for the definition of a good work ethic. That was my biggest mistake. I fell into the trap of the world that said that if my life was crazy busy then I was really living successfully. If things were chaotic, well, then I had a good thing going—my life mattered.

I once worked on a team that was overloaded, overrun, overburdened, and over *it*! Margin in our days and weeks had long since disappeared. We knew we had to make a change and so we did. We started working on a new team culture, and to keep us focused, we adopted a new mantra which we repeated over and over until we believed it: *Overworking is not noble.*

Thomas Merton said,

> Unnatural, frantic, anxious work, work done under pressure of greed or fear or any other inordinate passion, cannot properly speaking be dedicated to God, because God never wills such work directly. He may permit that through no fault of our own we may

> have to work madly and distractedly, due to our sins, and to the sins of the society in which we live. In that case we must tolerate it and make the best of what we cannot avoid. But let us not be blind to the distinction between sound, healthy work and unnatural toil.[12]

Adele Calhoun, in her book *Invitations from God*, says we don't have to justify our existence by "driving and striving."[13] We are created and loved unconditionally by God. Because of him, we are totally accepted and uniquely gifted. We don't need to *do* anything to *be* loved. We already are. The plan, then, is that we would act and *do* as an outpouring of our *being*. God is the source of who we are, our identity.

Abiding in him is what then shapes our daily life purposes and contributions. Our inner selves are strengthened by him, then poured out through the work of our hands. We aren't to live in such a way that our identities are contingent on our contributions. Our contributions, our purpose, our work, our love, and our lives are to pour out and overflow from our undeniable, uncompromised, unwavering identities given to us freely from the God of the universe. Calhoun encourages us to "set aside the compulsion to 'do, do, do' and live into God's creational rhythms that nourish and restore the body, soul, and relationships."[14]

Be ... then do. That's what we had to learn. That is God's transformational way.

Ahh ... Now I Understand Sabbath

Authors Marva Dawn (who wrote a book called *A Royal "Waste" of Time*—my first reaction was *why* would I want to do *that*?) as well as Abraham Herschel were really the ones to highlight the matter of *time* for me. They are experts on the spiritual practice of Sabbath. The Bible teaches about Sabbath and its place in the rhythm of life. Sabbath is a systematic day of rest in a period of time, and it is one of the Ten Commandments. That is a day to observe and remember the Lord.

Most Christians would say that Sunday is their Sabbath, a day to go to church and worship and a day off work. But just because it is a day off of work does not mean people don't often find themselves in a flurry of activity all day long. In fact, Sunday can be a very stressful, busy day for families. If so, then the truth is, it is not exactly a Sabbath. Really, Sabbath is hard to practice in a culture that never takes a break. Businesses work seven days a week. Stores are open all the time. The Internet is always available. We get pulled every which way 24/7.

But God says that Sabbath matters, and I want you to understand it. So, between Dawn and Herschel and my own exploration, the following is a thumbnail sketch of the need-to-know principles for how-to when it comes to practicing the Sabbath.

On the Sabbath we *cease.* We stop. We stop working, stop being productive, stop possessing, stop creating a way for ourselves. We stop so that we can make space for God's presence and purpose in our lives, trusting him to provide all we need.

On the Sabbath we *rest.* We let go. We rest physically, intellectually, and emotionally. We rest and let God reign. We are reminded that God is God, and we are not.

On the Sabbath we *embrace.* We hold close. We accept and hold close that which matters most to God (his heart becoming our heart) and accept and hold close God's will, whatever it may be (desiring him more than anything else). In this we reestablish that we are his and he is ours.

On the Sabbath we *feast.* We take in good things until we are full. We pray and play with God. We take in God's Word. We take in lots of joy. We do lots of whatever we love to do that will nourish our well-being. In this, we experience the goodness and love of God and are reminded of the abundant life he promised!

There is a myth that one cannot do anything on the Sabbath. People think you have to be still and quiet. But the truth is that any activity that is enjoyable and freeing and not undertaken for the purpose of accomplishment qualifies as acceptable for Sabbath time. The results of practicing the Sabbath are decreased anxiety, refocusing (on what really matters), renewing, and rejuvenating. Sabbath is actually a taste of eternity, and when we practice it, we anticipate heaven.

In case you didn't know it, God has rhythm. And when we are in step with him, we dance better. God takes time *to be.* You can, too.

Spiritual Pathways

In the ever-changing life of a Christian, there is nothing more essential than having a maturing, personal relationship with God. You are a unique expression of God, and your relationship with him is unlike any other. It really is *personal.* When you worship him, it is an intimate experience. Your voice is distinct to him. When you demonstrate adoration, praise, honor, and reverence to him, he knows it is you. And the clincher is that we all do that differently. We all have pathways of worship.

I first learned about pathways of worship from Gary Thomas in his book *Sacred Pathways.*[15] After studying Scripture, biblical people, and church history, he concluded that there are various expressions of worship that bring God glory. Good news for those who aren't much for music: singing is not the be-all and end-all when it comes to worship!

Finding your pathway of worship is essential to your ongoing spiritual transformation. Ask yourself these questions: How do I best connect with God? When do I feel closest to him? Where is his presence most evident to me? It is in this place or doing this thing that you take the most initiative and are most responsive to God. You worship God, you call him worthy in your heart, and you give him glory when you are *here*, when your hands are doing *this*. This is your pathway of worship.

Maybe you connect with God through the world that he has made, and being outdoors restores and energizes your relationship with him. Maybe holding the hands of others in a small circle of people is where you connect with God. Or you could be one who celebrates God with an enthusiastic shout and your hands raised! Is it symbols and liturgies that draw you closer to God? Or do you sense God's presence the most when your worship pathway is that of serving and your hands are reaching out, loving and helping others? Another pathway people don't always think about is that of the intellect—loving God with your mind. When your hands are filled with books and you are in stimulating discussion, you experience God in a powerful way. Or possibly, you are one who metaphorically holds a sword confronting injustice and evil, bringing God glory through your passion to act on his behalf for righteousness.

Whatever or however it is that you give God the glory that is his and worship him with your very being, that is what you ought to do. You do your part to keep your relationship with God strong, and he will do his. Let it bring you the greatest joy to know him in your very *being* and to worship him with all your *doing*.

Whisper 7: You Are a Unique Contribution to the World

God wonderfully and amazingly made you. He knows the number of hairs on your head. He knows your heart. He wired you with gifts and talents. You are the apple of his eye. If you never lifted a finger for a task in his name, all of this would still be true. You do not need to earn your way with God or to prove yourself to him. His love for you is unconditional. When you are simply *being*, he loves you. That's what makes the *doing* of life so good—we don't *have* to do it, we *get to* do it. As he pours into our being, he will overflow out of us to the world. When we go to work in his name, we are making a loving difference in the lives of others.

Yes, all believers are the hands and feet of Jesus. But our hands and feet are not cloned. We don't all act, live, and serve in the same way. I offer myself in one way; you offer yourself in another. With every different person, there is a needed expression of Jesus. It is so important that you understand who you are, what you do, and how you do it. You matter, and there is a reason you are here. People need your unique contribution to the world.

Whisper 8

Live Life with All Your Heart

Love and Passion

One Life

One life is what we are given, and it is a gift. It is easy in the day-to-day to forget the finiteness of it. But then something happens to someone else that touches us, and we are made tangibly aware that we are not promised tomorrow. There is an accident, a diagnosis, a suffering, or a loss; or a life hangs in the balance. During a time like this, we press a reset button for our lives. We determine that from that moment on, we will live more fully, taking nothing for granted. But just like New Year's resolutions, our rediscovered diligence for life fades—until the next tragedy comes by.

I have personally experienced and also witnessed this kind of rhythm in people's lives over and over. And for me, there came a point when I just had to decide that I wasn't going to count on the next tragedy to recalibrate and reignite my love and passion in life. I realized it was up to me to choose it daily; I had to keep that out in front of myself.

It isn't easy to do this kind of thing, but it is worth the effort. Can I say that I have lived every day of my life with a high score in love and passion? No. But I can say that I have lived *more* days with *more* love and passion than I would have if I hadn't made them a priority way of life for myself. Living with love and passion is not the easy road, but it is, by far, the most rewarding. Yes, you have to be vulnerable and put yourself out there. Yes, there are days when you have to sacrifice physically and emotionally beyond what you thought you had in you. True, we all need balance and reserves in our lives, but love and passion never store up too much; love and passion have to keep flowing. That's how it works.

Can I say I am like Christ? No. Far from that. But, I can say I am closer to becoming like him, because I asked him to be the one to teach me about what it means to truly live. He lived with love, and he lived with passion; he lived life with all his heart. And I want to do the same!

Kingdom Seeker

Loving God more than anything is the first step to the abundant life Jesus talked about. In 1985 singer/songwriter Twila Paris produced an album called "Kingdom Seekers" that I used to listen to over and over. There was a poster sold with a poem, and hung it in my room at home and then at college. In fact, I still have a scrap of it. It is a reminder of the early passion God gave me for him.

> There is a Kingdom
> That welcomes any pilgrim—
> A fortress high on a hill whose
> Brilliant light spreads over the whole earth.
> The sons and daughters
> Of the King are ransomed slaves—
> Grateful children who worship

Their loving Father.
They take great delight
In pleasing Him, and are
Constantly looking for ways to extend the borders of
His Kingdom.
They are called
Kingdom Seekers.

In college, a "kingdom seeker" was all I wanted to be through and through, and I hung out with people who wanted the same. We were committed Christians, open and willing to do anything and go anywhere, and as college students, we were in a prime position to do just that. We surrendered everything. We directed our majors toward ministry. Willing to give up the comforts of living in the United States if God called, we knew we might never live in our hometowns with families again. We understood that if we were going to live life with all our heart, God had to come first. We were seeking his kingdom and his righteousness and trusting him with everything else.

Though I dreamed of various roads I could travel and considered so many wonderful options in life, I knew then as I still do today that it was God who knew what was best. He had the all-knowing, all-present, all-powerful picture of the universe. I didn't. I wanted him to be first in my life and lead me in my life decisions. I recently found an entry in my journal from July 10, 1988, that said, "I want to live a million lives. But, you know, none of them would be worth it without Jesus. I choose to live the one life that God has given me, and to live it for Him." Even more so do I want that today. I want to love him most and live for him first.

Love, as mature people know, is not just a feeling; love is a choice. In life when we love someone, we must keep choosing to do so. Over time, I found that I had to keep *choosing* to love God. I could not put my love for God on an autopilot setting. Here is what

I mean. After college, when you get a job and a marriage and if you have some kids, life changes a lot, and it is easy to "settle in" to the American way. For me, from the beginning I would check myself every year to make sure I was where God wanted me, not settling into the norm "just because." I didn't want a happiness that resulted from a weekday job and weekend faith with an average compensation that provided for a lovely family—assuming these were just the given, automatic blessings of God. I wanted my joy to come from knowing that he had given me these things for a reason and put me there for a purpose. I didn't want to just live in a nice neighborhood cul-de-sac because I found it to be safe and comfortable. I wanted to know God had a plan. In that neighborhood, in my job, in my relationships I wanted to live fully *in* him and *for* him. I wanted to be a kingdom seeker, a grateful child of God, shining his love and light as bright as I could everywhere.

I still want that today. And so I still seek to love God most and first.

All My Heart

I want to be one who does things with all her heart. No holding back. No second-guessing. No halfhearted notions. I wanted to be devoted through and through, a pure heart engaged fully in living out her beliefs; praising God, trusting him, loving him, and serving him with an undivided heart. There used to be a little booklet called *My Heart, Christ's Home* sold in the wire roundabout at the Christian bookstore. It presented *the heart as a house* with many rooms: the kitchen, the library, the bedroom, the living room, etc. To read and pray through it was an exercise in *housecleaning of the heart*, the goal being to surrender any impurities or distractions in every area of one's life.

At age eighteen I traveled as a counselor to the retreat center where I originally came to know the Lord. There I was five years later, now in college, with my eyes open to what it really meant to serve in ministry as a volunteer and even possibly vocationally. I was learning how to share my faith effectively and felt the urgency of the Great Commission. That weekend was a milestone for me. People who had influenced my Christian life up until that point were there as well as new friends from my university. From both groups, in two separate moments, words were spoken into my life regarding a vocational calling to ministry.

That weekend was a surrender weekend. It was the weekend I gave God everything. None of my life belonged to me anymore. *I was his.* One of my playlist songs during that time of my life was by Steven Curtis Chapman called "Burn the Ships." It told the story of a Spanish fleet under the leadership of Hernando Cortés, which set sail in the spring of 1519 on a historical conquest to capture the treasures of Mexico. They landed on the eastern shore of Mexico with great dreams, but the hardships of the New World made them doubt, and they considered going back to the life they had known—it was easier! When Cortés got word of this, he commanded, "Burn the ships!" He resolved that they had not come this far to turn back. They had passed the point of no return—this was their home now. Retreat was not an option.

For those who are followers of Jesus, the story is similar. We have a new life, and sometimes the old life calls out "comfort" to us, and we want to go back to the life we lived and understood before we knew Christ. The path of least resistance is so often traveled when a crisis moment of choice like this comes. Yet, if we will stick with the new life God has given us and stay on course with him, he will do the things that we cannot yet imagine. We must call out, "Burn the ships," in our own life quest, being completely and totally committed to him with all our hearts.

Have you committed yourself to the Lord completely? Have you called out, "Burn the ships," in your own life?

Obedience

> And we can be sure that we know him if we obey his commandments. If someone claims, "I know God," but doesn't obey God's commandments, that person is a liar and is not living in the truth. But those who obey God's word truly show how completely they love him. That is how we know we are living in him. Those who say they live in God should live their lives as Jesus did.
>
> (1 John 2:3–6 NLT)

I have heard people say that they just don't feel like their relationship with God is strong. They say their walk with God is stagnant. They claim to be reading their Bibles, attending church regularly, and serving in a ministry, but they don't really feel they are growing. Looking for someone to blame, complaints about their current church usually follow.

After further discussion, it is usually discovered that though they are reading their Bibles and attending church services, they really aren't doing anything with what they are reading. If asked, they cannot account for the last time the Lord spoke to them and they acted on it. Plain and simple, lethargy has set in. You see, there is no active flow of the Spirit in our lives if we are not hearing the Word of God and doing the Word of God. If you are hearing only, it is getting stuck inside you, just sitting there. That's why they call people who lack obedience "fat Christians." You are just gaining spiritual weight sitting on the couch with your Bible rather than exercising your faith for the good of your soul and the good of others.

Listen, it comes down to one thing, and it is the one thing that no one wants to talk about: obedience. No one likes obedience. To talk about it with someone else is to judge them. To measure your life with it could result in legalism. But obedience is so much more than that. Obedience is saying yes to God for greater things. Obedience leads to a deeper relationship with God and a deeper faith. God is actively speaking to us through his Word, in our prayers, and through other believers, and when we hear him we must act—not ignore. Obedience is uncomfortable for the most part. That first step is awkward and there may be fear involved, but there is joy, reward, and fulfillment on the other side of saying yes.

Obedience is our responsibility. It is a decision we make. But we do it from a place of *dependence on God*—he makes a way for us to go his way. When we act in obedience, we take a step closer to the Lord and a step to becoming more like him. Oswald Chambers says, "Obedience is the means whereby you show the earnestness of your desire to do God's will. Through obedience you will receive, as a gift of God, this perfect adjustment of the personality of holiness—the life of Jesus Christ manifested in your mortal flesh."[16]

In other words, obedience is a key necessity to the transformational work God wants to do in us. It is not legalism or judgment. It is our affirming action that sustains our love for God and the flow of his Spirit in our ever-changing lives.

Noblemen and Noblewomen

I was at a conference when I heard a man share the following story, and it had a profound effect on me at the time. I have never forgotten it.

It was the Gulf War in 1991. As the first wave of airplanes headed out to Baghdad, a soldier piloted the plane whose target was the main power plant. If he hit his target, he would darken the city. He did it.

As he was preparing to retreat after completing that mission, an antiaircraft missile hit his plane. Punching his seat ejection lever, he was discharged out of the plane into the air and landed in a city street of Baghdad, unconscious. Shortly thereafter, he awakened while being carried along by the wind in his parachute. When he went to stand and hide, he found both his legs were broken, so he crawled behind some bushes. He activated the emergency satellite signaling device to alert the carrier, but the cloud cover prevented his rescuers from responding right away. Waking in the early morning light, he found himself hiding at the home of Saddam Hussein's elite guard. Two nights and two days he stayed awake with no food, falling asleep on the third night.

As he recounts the story, he says he dreamed about his past and his present (his childhood, school, money, joining the navy, dropping the bomb, getting hit by the missile). Suddenly, he was awakened by a hand on his shoulder shaking him and someone with a New Jersey accent saying, "Wake up, buddy. You're going home." Looking up to the night sky, he saw navy jets streaking in every direction, drawing enemy fire away from a lone helicopter hovering in the main intersection of Baghdad. The New Jersey navy man picked him up, carried him, and put him in the harness, and he was pulled up into the rescue copter. Because of this team of brave individuals, the soldier made it home.

Who were these heroes?

It was the 221st Squadron of US Navy Seals Search and Rescue Team—the elite of the elite. These are the ones who graduate in the top one percent of their class. They have no immediate living relatives. They are totally and completely committed to whatever the mission, and they think of only those they have been sent to rescue. They are called "The Noblemen." At the training center, above the exit door is a sign reading, "You have to go out. You do not have to return."

The speaker looked at us in the crowd and he asked us: "Will you be the noblemen and noblewomen of Jesus Christ? Will you respond to the distress signals that are being sent up by the spiritual prisoners of war, those who have been captured by the Enemy? Will you do whatever it takes to rescue them? For Christ's sake and God's heart, will you 'go out'?"

So, I ask you. When it comes to your passion for Christ and your love of people, will you engage with God's work in the world? Whether you live in an all-American cul-de-sac or take annual international mission trips, will you commit your entire life to being one of the noblemen and noblewomen for Jesus Christ?

Find a World

As a young college girl, I traveled on my first international mission trip. A few years later, I went again. Pretty soon I led a few trips with my husband for the youth group. Then, when I was employed full-time in vocational ministry, working for a church, I just couldn't seem to get away to go again. Upon pursuing my master's degree, I realized that I could not, for sure, travel anywhere until I completed all the course work! During the years that I studied and I worked, I was keenly aware of the potential of my "world vision" slipping away. I kept thinking to myself, *Self, do not get comfortable and forget about the world.* And I would say to the Lord, *Lord, as soon as this is done I will* go. And with that came the question, *Where* would I go?

Singer/songwriter Jami Smith produced a song that captured my heart: "Find a World." It was a lyrical expression of the Great Commission, and this song became my prayer: *Lord, help me find a world.* And after eight years of not traveling outside the United States, I traveled to the Philippines and there it was—my world. I can't say that I felt a special love or affinity for the country itself—it wasn't like that. But, what I knew in my heart of hearts was that God had an assignment for me there, a Great Commission kind of assignment.

It was the kind of mission that takes you out of your familiar Judea and into a world you never imagined. It is where you take the name of Jesus to people who have not heard and where you serve the poorest of the poor. The kind of mission where rather than just read about it, you meet people and make friends with those in the world who actually live on two dollars a day. The truth is, I can't imagine my life if I'd never found Mamatid.

Mamatid was the small town we traveled to where my friend Florante had a family plot of land. Born in the Philippines and now living in the States, he was the one who invited me to visit his hometown. When I agreed to go, I had no idea what I was in for. Five trips later with one church planted, a building constructed, and numerous medical clinics and feeding programs held, many lives were changed—primarily mine.

Being on mission in the Philippines has probably been the single most transforming experience of my life. Though the trips were short-term, the investment was long-term. By going there more than once and keeping in touch through technology, giving financially, and by offering ongoing emotional and prayerful support to the national leadership, I found myself an actual part of the living, breathing church in a far-off land. I preached at their weekend services, led worship, and trained their leaders. I was part of their weddings, and I watched their children grow up. People in that biblical community died, and I wept from my own personal loss of their friendship.

Over the years, I invited many of my friends to join me in the Philippines. Those who said yes were changed by the experience. God did a work in them they never expected, and they have their own stories to tell about it. I believe that God wants to do the same in you. I am not saying you need to go to the Philippines. In fact, I am not even saying that you need to go all that far. What I want to encourage you to do is fulfill the Great Commission in your own life, going the whole way to the end of those verses in Matthew 28:19–20. I want to encourage you to *find a world*. Go somewhere that is

- not your custom
- not your tradition
- not your language
- not your transportation
- not your music
- not your food
- not your weather
- not your fashion
- not your way of life

Maybe that's not five thousand miles away; maybe it is five miles. I don't know. What I do know is that being obedient to the Great Commission is part of living with love and passion. Jesus has his whole heart and being in this thing! We need to be in it with him! You will never be the same!

And just in case you are one who believes that Christians should be more concerned about doing good works in and taking the gospel to their own community rather than being involved in someone else's, I hope you will reconsider. The Great Commission says that both the near and far matter. The assignment to see the world transformed by the gospel of Jesus Christ starts at home, yes, but it then goes out … far out into the world (I believe Jesus mentioned the ends of the earth).

I, too, once wondered if I should travel across the seas to share about Jesus when there was so much work to be done around me. Upon that musing, God spoke to me through a devotional called *My Utmost for His Highest*, and I wrote this down in my journal: "If when God said 'Go' you stayed because you were so concerned about your people at home, you robbed them of the teaching and preaching of Jesus Christ Himself. When you obeyed and left all consequences to God, the Lord went into your city to teach; as long as you would not obey, you were in the way."

I took that seriously.

All In to the End

When I first starting vocational ministry, I served with a couple of guys who loved sports, especially football and baseball. And the key motivational phrase for the church staff team was, *Leave it all on the field*. We were in it to win it. We wanted to love people the way that God loved people, and we wanted to live with great passion serving him. We were not going to play it safe. We weren't going to hold anything back. We were putting it all out there, and everything was on the line. There were no hidden immunity idols in those days (for you *Survivor* fans).

In those days, "leaving it all on the field" was a little easier, I think. Life, though challenging, seemed a little clearer to me. Kind of like I knew what game we were playing and what field we were playing on. But things don't stay the same. As situations and circumstances began to change, over time I found it more difficult to play hard and give my all. Changes in life brought new teams and new playing fields. Clear, concise, fast-hitting thinking began to escape me and was replaced by slow, unsure swings at the ball.

Making it through the first seasons of real change in my adult life, I then realized that this would be a never-ending story; changes would always come. At that point I had to figure out how I would negotiate all the changes in life I would go through. And so I made a decision, adopted a policy, put a stake in the ground, made a declaration—however you want to say it. I decided that no matter what happened, I am *all in to the end.*

This is who I am, and this is who God calls me to be. I can slow down, doubt, or hesitate, but turning points are not stop signs. Intersections are not closed streets. God is here with me, and he is in this thing. Change does not elude him or confuse him. The destiny I'm looking for here on earth is not the ultimate destiny I need to be concerned about. I am a committed follower of God, and he directs my path.

Up until now, as best I could, I have lived with an "all-in" attitude. I arranged my time, talent, and treasure around his will as revealed to me through Scripture. And just because I am confused on occasion ... well, so what? Confusion does not justify apathy. The world can swirl around me. I may not know *what* I'm doing, but I am still going to live *how* God has shown me. I am all in to the end.

What about you? I want you to be all in to the end with me. No matter what happens. No matter what changes. No matter what our earthly eyes can or cannot see. We need to view life with spiritual eyes and live with spiritual hearts. He is forever faithful to us. Let us be forever faithful to him: all in to the end.

> So let's keep focused on that goal, those of us who want everything God has for us. If any of you have something else in mind, something less than total commitment, God will clear your blurred vision—you'll see it yet! Now that we're on the right track, let's stay on it.
>
> (Philippians 3:15–16 MSG)

Whisper 8: Live Life with All Your Heart

One of the unique blessings in my life was the opportunity to travel to the Middle East. Traveling there was less than safe and not a good idea at the time, but I was convinced I needed to go. On the night before I left, my mother signed the consent form under duress. I was already packing—I had left her no choice. With no money to take with me, my dad took me to the bank and gave me $200 in case of emergency. Yes, my parents, as well as the rest of my family and friends thought I was crazy.

On the trip we experienced the journey of the apostle Paul, the author of much of the New Testament. It was a wonder to me to set foot on the land where so much of the Bible was written. We went to such places as Hierapolis and Capernaum, Ephesus and Pergamum.

The city visit that had the most impact on me was that of Laodicea. In the other city ruins, there was stuff to look at. You could still see the imprint of an ancient city by the roadways, the shells of buildings, and the broken columns. But in Laodicea, there was nothing to see. It was kind of flat, dry, and brown with rubble scattered around. It seemed obvious that this was the city spoken of in the book of Revelation: the city where the Christians were indifferent. They were the church that was neither hot nor cold: they were lukewarm in their relationship with God. They did not live with love or passion for him.

At the end of our time there, I gathered up a handful of rubble and brought it back to the States with me. I remember standing in line at airport customs and realizing that those rocks might be a violation. They were already packed, and I didn't want to make a scene. I was nervous the whole way through! But, what can I say; to this day I'm glad I have that handful of rubble. Why? Because it reminds me that I don't want to be a lukewarm Jesus-follower. When I leave this earth, I don't want where I walked to be a dry and desolate place. I want my life to have mattered for God and his kingdom in such a way that God's living presence manifested in my ever-changing life makes an imprint on the world. I want people to walk by the cities in which I've lived and say, "Something happened here." So, I am going to do this thing—I am going to live life with all my heart. C'mon. You do it, too.

WHISPER 9

Let God Be God and You Be You

Feelings and Fear

Feelings Can Be Good

While faith is not a feeling, feelings do matter in our relationship with God. God created us with feelings, with emotions—in his image. Yes, God feels. Essential to our existence, feelings are the means by which we experience the fullness of life. They serve us in many ways when it comes to our ever-changing lives. Sometimes they can serve as a catalyst, creating turning points and opening up new directions. Always, feelings communicate. They are expressions of what we think. They are the method by which we can express our reactions. Feelings help us sense our surroundings, and they inform us and others what is happening in our hearts.

Feelings of joy and happiness are easily acknowledged and expressed, while feelings of sorrow and sadness ... not so much. Yet, those times when we are sad and sorrowful, times when our hearts are heavy need to be acknowledged. The old spiritual teachers called this *paying attention to your tears.* Simply, if we are crying, there is a reason, and that reason matters. It matters because it means that something is truly bothering us. We are hurting in some way.

More than what it means to us, it matters to God. He deeply cares about us. So, we need to pay attention to our tears and bring our hearts before the Lord so he can be with us, be for us, and restore us. He is the one who turns mourning into dancing, who makes beauty from ashes, and who understands our tears and can heal our hearts. He is the one who can actually comfort and console us and make us feel better when no one else in the room can. The Bible says that he is the one who will "restore the sparkle to [our] eyes" (Psalm 13:3 NLT).

Feelings Can Be Not-So-Good

It is said that while feelings are good servants, they are disastrous masters. My dad's advice was, "Never make a decision based on the mood you are in at the moment." It is a lesson I always appreciated. I have seen people take action based on a fleeting feeling, and they ended up with a permanent result they did not want. Feelings have to be managed, disciplined. They cannot roam free, and they cannot be in the driver's seat of your life. To understand your feelings and have them in their proper, healthy place in your life is a sign of maturity. It is immature people who allow feelings to rule the day.

Currently, we live in a world that says feelings are king. Magazine ads, television commercials, and radio spots play to our feelings so much so they compromise what is actually true. Reality TV shows produce hours of network television every week, intentionally pricking people's feelings and hoping for an outburst of anger, a quarrel, or a bad moral decision; the demise of the individual or group is the goal. Watching people mismanage their feelings and manipulate and hurt others has become good entertainment.

Dallas Willard says, "The mongoose of a disciplined will under God and good is the only match for the cobra of feeling.[17] We can't let emotions control us or paralyze us. We need to be aware of our circumstances, and we need to weigh the potential consequences with sound minds and discerning hearts, unclouded by feelings. Henri Nouwen says,

> One day we think we can take on the whole world, but the next even a little request seems too much for us. These mood swings show that we no longer hear the blessing that was heard by Abraham and Sarah; Isaac and Rebecca; Jacob, Leah and Rachel; and Jesus of Nazareth and that we, too, are to hear. When we are thrown up and down by the little waves on the surface of our existence, we become easy victims of our manipulative world, but, when we continue to hear the deep gentle voice that blesses us, we can walk through life with a stable sense of well-being and true belonging.[18]

Feelings: Are they servants? Yes. Masters? No.

Phantom Pain

Do you know anyone who has had a debilitating injury to a body limb where amputation was needed? Have you ever watched television on a topic like this? Sometimes the one who has experienced an amputation will swear he or she still feels the pain of that injury. Yet, the limb does not exist anymore. It is not even there. The field of medicine calls this "phantom pain."

The source of the pain does not actually exist anymore, but the brain has not caught up to that fact. For instance, have you ever had a splinter in your finger? It hurts! And so you get the tweezers and you take it out. Yet, sometimes days later it still feels like it's in there—but it's not. Have you been in a fender bender? It was scary! It's now been a year, but every time you approach that same intersection, your heart rate goes up, and you feel nervous. These are *kinds* of phantom pain.

I think phantom pain is more than a physical phenomena; I think we suffer from it emotionally, too. Here's what I mean: negative feelings seem to linger and are hard to get over. If you have been hurt in a personal relationship, if you have had a terrible boss, or if you were raised in a dysfunctional family, you may find that even though those things are over, the feelings they have left behind are troublesome.

You can tell you are suffering from phantom pain when an opportunity for a new relationship presents itself, but you are too afraid to engage with it. Or maybe you got a new boss, but instead of welcoming him or her, you have been obsessed with wondering if that person was going to be terrible like the last one. Or now, at the first sign of trouble in the family you are raising, you are freaking out with the fear that your childhood is going to happen all over again. Suffering with phantom pain means that though the situation has changed, you are living like it hasn't.

If my situation has changed, I must live with that truth. Living from a place of pain that no longer exists will stunt the growth God intends for me. I need to let things be solved and resolved. I need to let God make things new.

Do you know what I'm talking about? Is there any phantom pain in your life? You may have a deep hurt that has gone undealt with and requires some professional counsel. Or you may need some radical prayer. Or maybe you just need to acknowledge it and put it in the past where it belongs. Another way of dealing with emotional phantom pain is starving it until it dies—meaning, do not fuel it, do not feed it. Do not give it any thought or energy. Without nurturing, it will die like anything else. As it disseminates, you will be able to move on to what is real and new.

Feelings are hard to get over and hard to put in their healthy place. But you're going to have to if you want to keep yourself in an open posture for God to continue his work in you. Otherwise, your ever-changing life is going to get stuck in the past. Feelings, both good and bad, are part of who you are, and they cannot be ignored. Feel them. *You are you*—don't apologize for that. Let your feelings be and do all that they are designed for, and then manage them. Let your feelings serve you well.

Fear the Lord

You may have thought this section on fear was going to be about the kind of fear that says, "I am afraid." But this section talks about another kind of fear, the most important kind: fear of the Lord. If we will understand what it means to fear the Lord and then do so, the daily kind of fears we face will be no match for us anymore.

Understanding the fear of the Lord was a challenge for me in the beginning. And since then I have had many people ask me, what does it mean to fear the Lord? After all, he loves us, so why would we be afraid of him?

Fearing the Lord means to hold him high with reverence, worshipping him above all else, recognizing that his power is so mighty we cannot become comfortable with it. We stand in awe and bow down before him in humility. We live concerned about what God says rather than what man says, and we care more about what he thinks than what man thinks. We seek God's approval, not man's approval.

So if we fear the Lord, we will choose to listen to what he says, care about what he thinks, and seek his affirmation in our lives. At times we may think we or others know better, but it will be the fear of the Lord that keeps us listening to him. We may consider departing from the path of the Lord because we feel that we are better judges of our situations and the current culture, but it is the fear of the Lord that will keep us from straying. Our hearts may waver, but we will fear the Lord, and we will stay on the straight path. Within the fear of the Lord we will find knowledge, wisdom, and instruction. It is the fear of the Lord that will keep us away from evil and deception. It is the fear of the Lord from which true life will flow.

Respect and reverence. Authority and awe. Amazement and wonder. There is no one like him. Fear the Lord. Let God be God.

You be you.

Personal Holiness

My husband, Dave, always says this: "The greatest gift you can give someone is your own personal holiness."

> For God did not call us to be impure, but to live a holy life. Therefore, anyone who rejects this instruction does not reject a human being but God, the very God who gives you his Holy Spirit.
>
> (1 Thessalonians 4:7–8 NIV)

To live a holy life is to first and foremost be in relationship with the holy God. Jerry Bridges, in his book *The Joy of Fearing God* says that "progress in personal holiness must be built upon an ever-deepening awareness of God's holiness."[19] It does not mean we are flawless, but it does mean that because of Christ we are faultless, covered by his blood and the cross. It means we are people of truth. We live with dignity and integrity. We rail against having any duplicity within us, longing to be the same on the inside and outside, in private and in public. We are in pursuit of becoming like our Savior, Jesus Christ through and through.

> So think clearly and exercise self-control. Look forward to the gracious salvation that will come to you when Jesus Christ is revealed to the world. So you must live as God's obedient children. Don't slip back into your old ways of living to satisfy your own desires. You didn't know any better then. But now you must be holy in everything you do, just as God who chose you is holy. For the Scriptures say, "You must be holy because I am holy."
>
> (1 Peter 1:13–16 NLT)

Oswald Chambers makes an interesting statement saying, "Holiness, not love, is the greatest thing in the world: for holiness is the basis of love."[20] It is not something we might think of at first, on our own, but it does make sense. It was God's holiness that laid the foundation of his love. I hope this helps us understand the importance of holiness in our own lives. It is a personal holiness within us that will motivate us to deny ourselves and love others. It is personal holiness that will give us spiritual eyes to see life the way God sees it. It is his character in us that will develop an active lifestyle that emulates him and leads us to a life of love.

And just so we are clear, personal holiness is not something we earn. We are holy because God is holy, and we belong to him. That is grace. However, as Dallas Willard has pointed out over the years, grace is not opposed to effort. When you read the New Testament, you see how astonishingly energetic the apostle Paul is when he teaches about developing the new life God has given us. We are to take off the old life and put on the new; there is no suggesting that this will be done for us. As we have said before, God has a part and we have a part. Bridges says, "God ordains that we mature through personal diligence and effort, but He reserves to Himself the ability to make us grow. We're responsible to fan into flame the spark of the fear of God, but we're dependent on Him to make it happen."[21]

Personal holiness is our pursuit of God and the living out of his character within us. With an open heart and honesty, we pray that people would see God in us. We are not trying to be perfect, but we are seeking to be true. True to God, and true to ourselves. When others are not forced to guess who we are or *whose* we are—when they know that Jesus is at the center of our lives and we are living for him—they will relax in our presence, and in turn, experience his presence through us.

Purity

Oftentimes when the word *purity* is spoken, people freeze up. One, they are painfully aware that they are not pursuing purity. Two, they are secretly aware that they don't really want to. This is an expected tension in the Christian life. After all, our humanity is flawed; it is Christ who has made us pure through his blood and the cross. The Bible talks about the struggle between the old life before we knew Christ and the new life we have in him now. We are well aware of how we have fallen short of God's perfection, yet we are overjoyed that he has made a way of love and mercy!

Knowing that God wants to live in and through us, spirit and flesh, the Scripture offers insight and encouragement for us to pursue purity in both our inner lives and our outer lives. We want to live for Christ! We want to live the way he wants us to live! We long to please him. And we know that he cares about each of us having a pure heart and clear conscience. He desires us to have pure motives in all that we do. When he reads our minds, he hopes to see pure thoughts. The Scripture continually admonishes us to live a pure and blameless life, not for our own glory or purpose, but for his glory and purpose. Purity is not intended to be an intimidating or unattainable goal; it is to be a result of his Spirit living in us.

In today's culture, purity seems to have been relegated to the backseat of the Christian faith—by the church itself. The Christian community seems to see any discussion of purity as pharisaical. And not wanting anything to do with that, purity seems to be falling off the map of faith. What once were God-honoring choices are now viewed as outdated and lacking relevance. It used to be important to show that one's life was different because of Christ. Now, Christians spend a lot of their time trying to look the same as everyone else and blend into the world. Whereas it used to be a common act of love among the church members to deny ourselves freedoms so that someone else would not stumble, we now are more consumed with our *right* to exercise our liberties.

With all that said, I hope you know this: purity does still matter. We cannot forget that purity of mind and heart, word and deed is something the Bible commands, encourages, and hopes for believers. Remember? We are to be abiding in Jesus, allowing him to change us inside our skin, in our hearts and minds, so that we might be holy as he is holy, because of his blood and sacrifice. We live for more of his love to flow through us, transforming his holiness in us. We want to show the goodness of God, having no offensive way within us. Our hope is that people would see Jesus in us, free and clear. Our hope is that there would be no stumbling blocks or confusion to others experiencing an authenticity of faith that touches them through us.

Are you pursuing purity in your own life, or are you permitting things in your life that you know are not beneficial to you and your walk with God? I can tell you from experience: if you are entertaining impurities in your life, it is not and will not be worth it. At some point they will become a setback to your spiritual growth.

Cultivating Transparency

You know that book called *All I Really Need to Know I Learned in Kindergarten* by Robert Fulghum? That's the sentiment I hold for the ministry of Campus Crusade for Christ; everything I ever needed to know about life and ministry, I learned from them. In college I was part of that ministry. Our campus leaders were Marc and Patti Rutter. Along with so many other things, they taught us, more than once, about the importance and value of *cultivating transparency* in one's life.

The privilege of learning this early on in my faith was a greater gift than I probably understood at the time. Right from the beginning, I learned how to practice a Christian faith with an open heart and authenticity, without pretense. Being a Christian was not a *show.* At the time, this was particularly important because television evangelists were dominating the culture's perception of Christians through the use of mass media. And they were not representing Jesus well. There were always problems regarding power, sex, and money—all abused in the name of Jesus. Scandal after scandal. It made being a Christian complicated at times trying to explain it all away.

Since then, the tide has turned a bit. Transparency and authenticity are now popular in Christian circles. So popular, in fact, that they have sometimes trumped every other virtue of the Christian life. As a result, preachers are preaching from a more personal point of view, and believers share their stories more than ever. This is mostly a good thing. However, a dark side has revealed itself, too.

People have lost a sense of discretion when it comes to what is private, what is for small-group sharing, and what is for mass communication. Now, sometimes people just talk too much with too much information. TMI is authenticity run amuck. We need to be more self-aware in this and share appropriately.

On a another note, we can't ignore that the pressure to be more and more authentic has grown to the point where people have started making up stories to make themselves *look real*. Meaning, people have started making sin bigger in their lives than it actually is. People are faking desperation, dramatizing stuggles, and creating history that doesn't exist in order to appear more troubled in this life than they actually are. It's kind of like the mentality of keeping up with the Jones when it comes to materialism; Christians are trying to keep up with other Christians when it comes to being authentically spiritual. Instead of wanting people to see that my house is *bigger* than theirs, I want them to see that my problem is *worse* than theirs - an "I need Jesus more than you do" throw down. We need to guard against this.

Cultivating transparency in the Christian life is a willing acknowledgment that following Jesus is by no means a perfect or easy life. It means that we pull back the curtains of what we are thinking and doing, being honest about our successes and struggles in our own spiritual growth. There is no need to appear superspiritual to others. We can nurture honesty and truthfulness in our lives through conversation and relationships that are genuine and real. I encourage you to do that.

Faithfulness Matters

God loves redemption. He loves to see someone's life changed by his cross. He is all about it. He gave his all to it. And God loves faithfulness. He commands us to it and empowers us for it. He desires that we be devoted to him above all else. It brings him joy to see our love for him lived out in faithfulness.

He loves both. In the Scripture, side by side, he speaks words and tells stories about redemption and faithfulness. Both are his story. Both are our story. Over and over again, he continues to write these two things in the lives of people.

However, I'm not sure we love and appreciate both. It seems to me that because people today love good stories so much, the church has begun to highlight exciting stories of redemption more than boring stories of faithfulness. Much more. A redemption story has dramatic qualities in it. It has a big moment. There is a before, a climax, and an ending—or, better said, a new beginning. But a story of faithfulness or sanctification is a long-haul story that goes pretty slow. It is a story written over time. Much time.

So, what I want you to hear is this: faithfulness matters. Do not be bored by the ongoing work of the Spirit in your life. As you live each day, embrace all the changes God brings about around you and in you. True, most days you may not even know it's happening, but God is developing a personal holiness within you. He *is* changing you to become more like him. And you know what? It *is* thrilling! There *is* a grand beginning, middle, and ending to the story, and when it is all said and done, you will see there were *countless big moments!*

Whisper 9: Let God Be God and You Be You

In your ever-changing life, understanding your role and understanding God's role will make all the difference when it comes to your personal growth. You don't have to fake it to make it; you need to know that it is okay for you to be you, authentic and true. At the same time, you need to let God be God. Understand who he is, worshipping him in spirit and truth. Be faithful. Pursue purity. Open up your heart in daily surrender for his love and holiness to develop in you.

Whisper 10

Move and Motivate Your Soul

Creativity and Inspiration

Two Needed Things

Creativity and inspiration are often considered impractical and intangible. I get that. But make no mistake: if you take a long, clear look at the world before you, you will find that creativity and inspiration are at the core of almost everything. It is new ideas and original thoughts that bring both beauty and board meetings to life. It is creativity that inspires and brings about change, action, and transformation. It is creativity that solves political matters and logistical issues as well as moves the heart and mind to new perspectives and horizons.

Creative methodologies stir up systems and bring about needed innovations. Creative contributions of every kind inspire faith and hope among nations of people while building bridges of love. Artistic masterpieces like paintings, stories, sculptures, pictures, dramas, and songs communicate values and thoughts that might go unspoken. All of this and more move and motivate the soul.

Inspiration

Each one of us needs inspiration. It is a necessary piece of life. Though a catalyst for change, it can be hard to come by sometimes. Inspiration is invisible, a bit of a mystery to be captured. It is not something that can be drummed up or forced, and it can be hard to put your finger on it. But even so, we can't sit around waiting for it to breeze by and hope we don't miss it. We need to be intentional about inspiration.

At the least, you first need to identify some of the things that you know inspire you. Sure, inspiration often comes in surprising places and packages, but the fact is, you are wired to be inspired by certain things. You already know what those things are. Music? Visual art? Prose? Stories? Theater? Nature? People? Information? Adventure? Sports? What moves and motivates your soul? What is it that evokes emotion within you and makes your heart feel full? What is it that leaves you feeling changed when it is over? What is it that after hearing it, seeing it, or doing it, makes you ready to take on any challenge? What, who, where, etc., inspires you to rise up and be your best *in* and *for* the world?

Second, when you know what inspires you, you need to get yourself inside that space, no matter the cost. As a pastor of artists, one of the line items in my church budget was *Inspiration.* Why? Because people need inspiration for themselves before they can go on to inspire others. And because it was a priority, I set aside the needed funds to be sure that it happened for the lead artists in the church.

Front-row concert tickets? Orchestra seats for the theater? Canvas and paint? Good books? Conference registration? A day at the coast? Skydiving? Whatever made the artist tick, I tried to make it happen for him or her. Of course, inspiration does not always cost money; sometimes it costs only time and energy. Either way, if inspiration is going to be a priority in your life—and I think it should be—then you should plan on investing in it, whether pricey or free. It is worth it.

The Why and How of Inspiration

On occasion a financial analyst would come across my budget line item "inspiration" and have some probing questions for me. Essentially, he or she wondered if money was being ill spent on *fun*. (God forbid—we wouldn't want that!) At that point I would have to let them in on a little secret that apparently they were not aware of: inspiration wages war on passivity. I explained to them that since inspiration moves and motivates people, productivity increases. I reminded them that vision leaks and teams drift south, and it is inspiration that fills up and fuels the vision tank and spurs the team upward again.

The same is true for individuals. It is easy for us to become passive in our pursuit of life. In the midst of our own spiritual formation—while God is doing a work within us—we can get lazy. We can get sluggish and begin to settle for less than God has for us, and we will become spiritual couch potatoes if we let "drift" happen for too long. Our changing lives necessitate that we make a priority of inspiration, for it is the intangible, wondrous, invisible God-gift that moves and motivates our souls.

Inspiration must be maximized. Sometimes inspiration can leave one with great feelings, but nothing ever happens as a result. The truth is that inspiration is at its best when it is paired with information. If inspiration comes without information, well, people really are not sure how to proceed. They are ready to act but aren't sure how. Inspiration alone will just end up sitting there and eventually fading. It is information and application that maximize the influence of inspiration. These put inspiration into motion. So, when you feel inspired, don't let it sit alone. Nurture and nourish it with action. Whatever new thing God is doing in your life at the time, apply inspiration to it and take the next step, risk it, go for it, and make it count.

For Me, It Is the Sound of Music

I am an artist, and I love any kind of art. Paintings captivate me. Pictures speak volumes to me. Stories evoke unspoken emotion in my heart. Theater transports me. But more than anything else, I love music—specifically, I love songs. Songs are almost like people. They are individuals with personalities. They have a message.

Throughout my life, music has been the number one art form that has inspired me. I could not imagine my life without music. It makes me, breaks me, molds me, and moves me. In light of this awareness, it is necessary for me to be sure music is part of my life. Being too busy to listen to music is not an option, because in the end, it is music that God uses to move and motivate me in whatever I am busy doing.

I enjoy, what I call, *the first listen.* When a singer or songwriter comes out with a new release, I savor the first time I get to hear those songs. I only get to hear them for the first time, one time. So, I make the most of it. I plan a time and place for it, and I take it in.

I believe in the power of a playlist. In fact, before there was such an actual thing as a playlist, I had one. For my whole life since I can remember, I had songs that were significant to me. Inside my journals of the past I listed songs that mattered, quoted the lyrics, wrote about how they made me feel, took notes on what I learned from them, and talked about how the Lord spoke to me through the song.

Collecting these songs on my iTunes, I have a playlist called "Kim's Journey." ("Kim," because when I started my Christian walk, everyone called me Kim—*Kimberly* came later.) This playlist has songs that still stand out for me as ones that inspired and formed my faith (and they are not all necessarily Christian songs). These are the songs that drew me into the presence of God, and the songs that were pertinent to my decision-making at the time, and songs that marked life events: milestone songs.

Why? Because music helps me remember how the Lord has been with me already in this life, and it gives me faith that he will continue to be with me. Music gets my spirit soaring and believing that I can do anything in this life! Music raises my pulse and spikes my blood pressure in a good way: it brings me to life. I have to have it. God wired me for it and it for me.

And since I am still a work in progress, I keep adding to that playlist.

Creativity

Creativity is often the originator of inspiration. When you look at Scripture, you realize how creative God is, even beyond the Genesis account. He used images as symbols to communicate with people. The pillar of cloud. The pillar of fire. A dove. The lamb. He is a doorway, the bread, the vine. In Scripture, colors matter and architecture has meaning. Even now, you can probably think of images and symbols that communicate to you the presence and power of God.

Made in the image of the Creator, we all have creativity in our DNA. Sure, some people are gifted in creativity; there are truly talented artists in genres of various kinds. But all of us *create* as a way of life; we just don't always think of it that way. It is a beautiful thing to simply *make* something. There is something therapeutic that happens in the soul when we do so. You have probably never thought of it this way, but there is a reason that craft stores, tool shops, and HGTV are so popular—we are a creative people!

Creativity in its finest form does not exist for its own sake. Creativity is at its best when it is *giving* to others. Creativity that contributes is powerful. It would be my hope that we all live out our God-given creative nature. When the creativity that resides in people comes out, we have the opportunity to foster extraordinary moments inside ordinary hours for those within our reach. And as God moves and motivates our own souls, he uses those moments to move and motivate the souls of others.

We Inspire Each Other

I come from a family of creative expression. Some were actually artists and some were not—it didn't matter. My aunts and uncles were always making something. One was a clay worker on a potter's wheel; he had his own art show at a gallery in the big city. Another was a fantastic portrait and mural painter, often hired for her expertise. One was a seamstress of the finest fabrics in the world. And my closest great-aunt could play the piano like nobody's business; she was once recognized by Liberace himself. And in the midst of all these, summer after summer, my grandfather created the best-decorated lawn with the most ornaments of anyone I have ever met.

From each of them I learned much about the power of creativity and art. First, it was fundamental to their well-being. They *needed* to do it. The activity of it moved and motivated them in every aspect of their lives. Second, it was vital to the well being of others. I watched so many people be moved and motivated by what they shared through their creativity. In my case, I am forever grateful to musicians who eat and breathe music—sacrificing everything for it—never dreaming of doing anything else.

Athletes. Actors. Songwriters. Singers. Potters. Painters. Architects and interior designers. Home crafters of every kind. All of these and more have the potential to inspire us. Sometimes it is the quality and expertise of the art that captures us. Sometimes it is the message being communicated. Sometimes it is the personal connection that we have with the one who actually did *the making*. And sometimes, it is us—something *we* have made (that may or may not be worthy in our own eyes) but that someone ... somewhere ... some way is inspired by an expression of the creator God in us.

We must keep inspiring each other however the Lord gifts us and leads us to do so. There is nothing like being a part of the process that moves the heart and soul of another. It is magical. Yes, magical.

Whisper 10: Move and Motivate Your Soul

The necessity of motivation can't be minimized. When we are not motivated, we are only doing things out of duty. And while duty is honorable and sometimes needed for follow-through when we don't feel like finishing something, it is no way to live. God does not want us to follow him out of sheer duty that is filled with drudgery and waning interest. When we met him, he changed our lives! And now he has invited us to an ever-changing life, one of adventure, meaning, and beauty. Keeping alert and on point with God will require an ongoing tank fill-up of inspiration and creativity so that our motivational engines keep humming strong and long. So do it. This is the fun part. Move and motivate your soul!!!!!!!!!!

Conversation Guide

This section has questions for reflection and guidance. It is intended for use in conversations between you and God, and between you and others.

Whisper 1: Embrace and Experience Every Day of Your Life: Moments and Seasons

- Can you see the role moments and seasons play in your ever-changing life?
- What moments in your life changed how you think?
- What moments in your life changed how you act?
- What seasons in your life have been the most profound? What did you learn from them? During those seasons, what transformations did the Lord do in you?

Whisper 2: Remember, You Are Never Alone: Presence and Wonder

- Can you see how presence and wonder matter to your transformation?
- Do you suffer from SADD: Spiritual Attention Deficit Disorder?
- Did you experiment with either of Leighton's applications (looking long enough or looking freshly at what is familiar)? Talk about it.

- Do you ever feel alone? Talk with the group about what you might do to remind yourself of God's presence always with you.
- Talk about the wonder of God. Where have you seen it? How have you experienced it? Has it played any role in God's transformative work in your life?

Whisper 3: Pay Attention to Where You Are and Who You Are With: People and Places

- Can you see how people and places matter in the transformational process?
- Who is sitting in your Kiss and Cry section?
- Do you have any balcony people in your life?
- Who is on your team?
- Who is your mentor?
- Are you invested in a local church? If so, how has it benefited your walk with Christ? If not, would you reconsider after reading this chapter?
- Do you have any sacred places that are markers in your journey of faith so far?
- Do you have a sacred space where you meet God during the week or on some regular basis?

Whisper 4: God Sees You Even If You Can't See Him: Darkness and Doubt

- How can you see that darkness and doubt can be significant to your spiritual formation?
- Have you ever experienced the Lord as your shelter, your shadow, or your shield? Did you know it then or are you just realizing it now? Share your story.
- Have you ever struggled with doubt? Explain.

- Do you have trouble resting in the fact that God sees you even when you can't see him?
- What does it mean to you to know that God can always see you, knows what you are going through, and will love you unconditionally?

Whisper 5: God Knows You Better Than You Know Yourself: Beloved and True

- Can you see how your identity in Christ matters to your personal formation?
- Have you ever struggled with self-rejection? How?
- In what ways do you try to earn your identity?
- What would it look like if you believed you were chosen and invited to live as the beloved? Describe what your daily thoughts and actions would be.

Whisper 6: Take a Step: Sin and Struggles

- What are the temptations you face in life? How can you be proactive in resisting them?
- Has there been a time in your life when sin derailed you and hindered growth in your relationship with God? Are there any sinful behaviors you are dealing with in your life right now? Do you have any secrets? What step do you need to take?
- Do you have a current wound of the heart that needs healing? How is it hindering your spiritual formation? What step do you need to take?
- Share a story where you have extended forgiveness or received forgiveness. Describe if and how this has been part of God's transforming work in you.

Whisper 7: You Are a Unique Contribution to the World: Being and Doing

- Do you or have you ever suffered from hurry-sickness? What did you or are you going to do about it?
- Are you taking enough time *to be* in your life?
- Do you practice Sabbath principles at all? Does your life have a rhythm or is it a full-court press all the time? Does anything need to change?
- How would you describe your unique contribution to the world? What do you bring to the world, to others around you? Talk about the passions God has put on your heart. Talk about the gifts and talents he has given you. How do those two things match up for your unique contribution?

Whisper 8: Live Life with All Your Heart: Love and Passion

- Are you living with love and passion right now? In what ways are you doing well and living life intentionally? In what ways do you want to improve your passion factor?
- Would you consider yourself a *kingdom seeker*?
- Have you committed yourself to the Lord completely? Have you called out "burn the ships" in your own life?
- What are your next steps when it comes to *finding a world*?
- Have you ever met someone who was a nobleman or noblewoman for Christ in the sense of the story told? Talk about them.

Whisper 9: Let God Be God and You Be You: Feelings and Fear

- Do you allow emotions and tears to be a part of your life, or do you stuff your emotions and hide your tears?
- How are you at managing your feelings?

- What makes you laugh? What give you hope? What makes you cry? What makes you feel free? What weighs you down?
- Do you have a healthy understanding of what it means to fear the Lord?
- Are you intentionally pursuing a personal holiness?
- What transformation are you hoping most for God to do in your life?

Whisper 10: Move and Motivate Your Soul: Creativity and Inspiration

- Can you see how creativity and inspiration matter to your transformation?
- In what areas of your life does the spirit of creativity flow from you?
- When you want to be inspired, what do you need? Where do you go? What do you do?
- Are you making room for and investing in inspiration in your life?
- Describe two of the most memorable times of inspiration when your soul was truly moved, and you were different as a result.

Endnotes

1. Bruce Wilkinson, *Secrets of the Vine* (Sisters, Oregon: Multnomah, 2001).
2. Leighton Ford, *The Attentive Life: Discerning God's Presence in All Things* (Downers Grove, IL: IVP Books, 2008), 119.
3. A. W. Tozer, *The Pursuit of God* (Camp Hill, PA: Christian Publications, 1982), 36.
4. Ford, 37.
5. Ibid., 38.
6. Jacki Hudson, *Doubt: A Road to Growth* (San Bernardino, CA: Here's Life Publishers, 1987), 91.
7. Henri Nouwen, *Life of the Beloved* (New York, NY: The Crossroad Publishing Company, 1992), 33.
8. Eugene Peterson, *Run with the Horses* (Downer's Grove, IL: IVP Books, 1983), 38.
9. David Benner, *The Gift of Being Yourself* (Downers Grove, IL: IVP Books, 2004), 104.
10. Thomas Merton, *New Seeds of Contemplation* (New York, NY: New Directions Publishing, 1972), 161.
11. Ibid.,32.
12. Ibid.,19.
13. Adele Calhoun, *Invitations from God* (Downers Grove, Illinois: IVP Books, 2011), 20.
14. Ibid.

15. Gary Thomas, *Sacred Pathways* (Nashville, TN: Zondervan, 1996).
16. Oswald Chambers, *Devotions for a Deeper Life* (Cincinnati, OH: God's Bible School, 1986), kindle.
17. Dallas Willard, *Renovation of the Heart* (Colorado Springs, CO: NavPress, 2002),127.
18. Nouwen, 73.
19. Jerry Bridges, *The Joy of Fearing God* (Colorado Springs, CO: Waterbrook Press, 1997), 66.
20. Chambers, kindle.
21. Bridges, 120.